SMALL BITES

SMALL BITES

MINDFULNESS FOR EVERYDAY USE

Annabelle Zinser

PARALLAX
PRESS

Berkeley, California

Parallax Press
P.O. Box 7355
Berkeley, California 94707
www.parallax.org

Parallax Press is the publishing division
of Unified Buddhist Church, Inc.

Cover and text design by Gopa&Ted2,Inc
Cover image © Thinkstock
Author photo © Janina Egert

Library of Congress Cataloging-in-Publication Data

Zinser, Annabelle, 1948-
  Small bites : mindfulness for everyday use / Annabelle Zinser.
    pages cm
  ISBN 978-1-937006-24-2 (pbk.)
  1. Meditation. 2. Awareness. I. Title.
  BF637.M4Z56 2013
  294.3'444—dc23

                                          2012040876

1 2 3 4 5 / 17 16 15 14 13

Contents

Introduction

THIS BOOK is designed to be read in small bites. Open it wherever you are, even if you only have a moment, and you will find a meditation that will hopefully bring some more joy into that moment.

Many of us associate meditation with sitting, still and relaxed. This is a central aspect of Buddhist meditation called stopping, *shamatha* in Sanskrit. Another aspect of Buddhist meditation is focused on insight, *vipashyana* in Sanskrit. We may try to see a difficult situation with more clarity, or we may contemplate the essential nature of our existence —that everything is impermanent, empty of a separate self, and interconnected with all things, what Vietnamese Zen Master Thich Nhat Hanh calls "interbeing"—with a goal of understanding these concepts on a deeper level.

The guided meditations in this book offer both opportunites for stopping and opportunities for insight.

They are based on insights that have come from my many years of studying with Thich Nhat Hanh, and the Buddhist teachings. These meditations are meant to support you as you practice in daily life. I hope they will help you to:

▸ Live more mindfully.

▸ Increase awareness so that you're able to notice the smaller and greater joys and the miracles of life.

▸ Handle physical and emotional pain so that you suffer less.

▸ Recognize and transform difficult emotions like fear, anger, despair, insecurity, jealousy, and depression.

▸ Cope more skillfully with the ups and downs of life.

▸ Nourish beneficial states of mind like goodness, joy, compassion, generosity, appreciation, and equanimity and ask them to manifest more often.

▸ Understand that you're not an isolated individual, but that you're connected with everything that exists on our planet and in the cosmos.

We all experience some suffering in our lives. My hope is that the meditations in this book will ease that suffering by helping you to:

▸ Recognize when you suffer.
▸ Recognize the conditions that have led to your suffering.
▸ Know that there is the possibility of transforming your suffering.
▸ Understand and practice the elements of the Buddha's Noble Eightfold Path, which leads to well-being and the transformation of suffering.

These meditations can be practiced either alone or in a group. When you practice on your own, you can read the introduction to the meditation, then be aware of your breathing for a few minutes, and then read the first two lines of the meditation. While the words penetrate, let your breath flow naturally. Allow thoughts and feelings to come and go. Don't have any expectation of achieving a particular mental state. Keep coming back to the awareness of your breath Then read the next phrase. You can also create your own guided meditations to fit whatever situation you might find yourself in.

When you practice mindfulness in daily life, you can more easily choose which energies to bring into your consciousness. This will support you in leading a more peaceful and happy life. You will also begin to notice which energies you might want to transform.

When you practice the meditations, there's no need to follow the suggested order. You can choose the guided meditation that speaks to you at that time. You may want to practice it for a few days or more.

When you practice with a group, the person leading the meditation may read the introduction and add his or her personal experiences connected with the topic of that guided meditation. We begin each guided meditation by inviting three sounds of the bell. First we invite a short sound of the bell to prepare the listeners for the full sounds that will follow. As you listen to each sound of the bell, take time for at least three deep and relaxed breaths.

As the sound of the bell fades, continue to follow your breathing, become aware of your whole body, and bring peace and relaxation to your body as you breathe in and out for several minutes. The group leader will read the first two phrases aloud. Let the words penetrate, and observe the effect of the words on your body and mind as you breathe in and out. Never force your breathing; always breathe naturally.

Simply being aware of your breathing allows it to become deeper, slower, and more relaxed on its own.

Taking time at the end of each meditation for a thoughtful exchange with each other can be very beneficial. You can each share your experience with the practice and how the meditation might have touched you.

These contemplations are simple yet they can be tremendously beneficial. If you take good care of yourself, you'll begin to feel more loving, peaceful, and stable, and this will have a positive effect on others as well. You'll begin to truly be there for yourself and for those with whom you share your life: your partner, children, parents, other family members, friends, coworkers, and also strangers. Your own practice of mindfulness, concentration, and deep understanding will give you the stability needed to fully participate in your family, your community, and in the world.

I wish you great joy in your practice.

1

Sitting Meditation

WHEN PRACTICING sitting meditation, it's important to have a supportive cushion. Sitting should be comfortable, not painful. If a cushion isn't comfortable or supportive enough, you can use a meditation bench or a chair. If you sit on a cushion, you can put one foot on the opposite thigh, both feet on the opposite thighs, or simply sit cross-legged. When sitting on a cushion, your knees should touch the floor; if they don't, you can support each knee with a small cushion. If you choose to sit on a chair, try not lean back in the chair. Sit with your spine straight, your knees relaxed, and your feet flat on the floor or on a cushion.

Always sit with a relaxed and straight spine. This will make your posture stable. Be sure your position is comfortable and relaxed. You may want to slightly lower your chin to avoid creating tension in your neck. You can rest your hands on your thighs with palms up or down, or else one on top of the other in your lap with palms facing up. Other options are to interlock your fingers in a prayer position or to use a basic *mudra*, hand gesture, in which the thumbs and index fingers, or thumbs and middle fingers, touch. The most important thing is to find a comfortable and relaxed position.

As you maintain awareness of breathing in and out, let your breath flow naturally without trying to influence it. Your breath may be long or short, shallow or deep. Simply notice it and observe it. Become aware of your abdomen expanding as you inhale and contracting as you exhale. Become aware of the contact of your legs or your feet touching the floor. Feel the floor and the cushion or chair supporting you. Be aware of your shoulders and arms and the position of your hands, and allow them to relax.

If your mind starts to wander, you can gently acknowledge this by naming it: "This is daydreaming," or, "This is thinking." Then return to your breathing. Rejoice in every conscious in-breath and out-breath. Don't fight with your mind. Meditation doesn't mean that you turn yourself into a battlefield. Just enjoy the degree of concentration that's possible in this very moment.

To help develop concentration, some people like to count their breaths from one to ten. You can make an in-breath number one and an out-breath number two. Or you can make one in- and out-breath number one and the next number two. Just count in whatever way is most natural for you. You can count to ten this way and then start over again. Or you may silently say "in" as you breathe in and "out" as you breathe out. Once in a while, you might acknowledge the noises around you and focus your mind by simply listening. Counting or naming are tools that help keep the mind focused on your breathing. You also want to become aware of the feelings that arise as you breathe in and out. If you feel pain in your knees or back, you can adjust your sitting position slowly and quietly in order to not disturb others. But before changing position it's helpful to explore the painful area and see how the pain changes as you inhale and exhale. (See "Opening Up to Physical Pain," p. 96)

At the beginning or end of the meditation, you can

repeat one phrase or several loving kindness phrases directed toward yourself or toward others. You may say:

May I be peaceful, happy, and at ease in body and mind.

You can also dedicate your meditation to someone close to you, or to another person or group of people who are suffering. You can send them your wishes for their well-being:

May you be peaceful, happy, and at ease in body and mind.

May your pain give rise to greater compassion for yourself and others.

When you adopt a meditation practice it's important to begin with the amount of time that suits your needs and schedule. You may start by sitting for five or ten minutes and then gradually sit for longer periods as you get more comfortable with the practice. You may eventually extend the time to twenty, thirty, or forty-five minutes. If you start out by sitting for too long, you might drop your practice after a few weeks because it's too big a commitment. That would be a pity, because then you would lose contact with this wonderful, ancient practice that's brought healing to so many people. However, it is important that you practice sitting meditation on a daily basis in order to develop a certain rhythm and skill in your practice. This is the only way you'll be able to harvest the fruits of your practice: greater openness, serenity, joy, peace, mindfulness, concentration, deep understanding, and insight.

2

Focusing the Mind

WHEN YOU SIT DOWN to meditate and actively focus your mind on the present moment, you develop an open awareness of the movement of your breath, the position of your body, the noises around you, and your feelings and thoughts. You don't reject anything, your mind doesn't cling to anything, and you don't long for anything, except for what is happening in the present moment, and you take in what is.

Another method of focusing the mind is to contemplate a single object. It might be your breathing, a guided meditation phrase, or an image of a Buddha or a bodhisattva. By focusing on a single object, your thoughts, plans, worries, and difficulties can fade away in a moment. For example, when you focus on the movement of your breath, you begin to notice which phases of your in-breath and out-breath escape your attention. You might then give special attention to these phases, so that your observation of the whole length of our breath improves. The goal is for you and your breath to sit together until there is only breath. To do this takes practice. Each moment you sit, guide your wandering mind back to your chosen object again and again.

*Aware of my breath, I feel my abdomen rising
and falling. Aware of my breath…oh, I mustn't
forget to put Bettina's flyer into the display case…*

*Aware of my breath. I feel my body relax…
oh, I have to remember to call the electrician to
fix the door bell…*

Each time you guide your mind back to your breath. Each time you come back, it creates more space and peace in body and mind. Simply notice where your mind is dwelling and guide it gently back to your breath. It's important to realize that wandering from one thought to the next is a natural function of the mind. If you get upset or judge yourself for having thoughts during a meditation session, the inner peace that you long for will always elude you. Here

are a few simple questions you may ask yourself to
help keep the mind focused on the flow of the breath:

*Can I feel the full length of the in-breath and the
out-breath?*

Can I feel joy in this one in-breath and out-breath?

*Can I be at peace with the amount of concentration
I'm experiencing right now?*

The following guided meditations can help you
maintain selective or active concentration during
meditation.

SELECTIVE CONCENTRATION

*Breathing in, I'm aware that I'm breathing in.
Breathing out, I'm aware that I'm breathing out.*

*Breathing in, I'm aware of the full length of my
in-breath.
Breathing out, I'm aware of the full length of my
out-breath.*

*Breathing in, I notice how my mind escapes into
thoughts and dreams.*

Breathing out, I guide my mind back to my breath.

Breathing in, I'm aware of my whole body.
Breathing out, I calm my body.

Breathing in, I give attention to the part of my in-breath that escaped my observation earlier.
Breathing out, I'm aware of the full length of my out-breath.

Breathing in, I feel the full length of my in-breath.
Breathing out, I give attention to the part of my out-breath that escaped my observation earlier.

Breathing in, I allow my breath to flow naturally without influencing it in any way.
Breathing out, I notice how my breath is changing just by paying attention to it.

Breathing in, I enjoy every in-breath.
Breathing out, I enjoy every out-breath.

ACTIVE CONCENTRATION

Breathing in, I'm aware of my in-breath.
Breathing out, I'm aware of my out-breath.

Breathing in, I'm aware of my whole body.
Breathing out, I calm my whole body.

Breathing in, I'm aware of all the
physical sensations.
Breathing out, I'm aware of all the
physical sensations.

Breathing in, I notice the sounds around me.
Breathing out, I notice the sounds around me.

Breathing in, I open myself to receive this in-breath.
Breathing out, I open myself to listen to the sounds
around me.

Breathing in, I'm aware of a thought.
Breathing out, I know this is just a thought.

Breathing in, I'm aware of the coming and going
of my thoughts.
Breathing out, I'm aware of the coming and going
of my thoughts.

Breathing in, I'm aware of the preciousness
of my practice.
Breathing out, I smile to myself.

3

The Four Foundations
of Mindfulness

IN THE SATIPATTHANA SUTTA, the Discourse on
the Four Foundations of Mindfulness, the Buddha
identifies four areas of self-observation: body, feelings,
mind, and objects of the mind.[1]

The first foundation of mindfulness is the body,
which includes the five senses of sight, hearing, smell,
taste, and touch. In sitting meditation, you focus on
the breath and observe the physical sensations in the
body.

The second foundation of mindfulness is the feelings. Bring your awareness to your feelings and notice whether they are pleasant, unpleasant, or neutral.
You might notice a tendency to hold on to pleasant

1. From Majjhima Nikaya (No. 10), the second of the five books of
Buddhist scripture in the Sutta Pitaka of the Pali Canon. The Canon
contains more than 10,000 discourses attributed to the Buddha or his
close companions.

feelings of body or mind, and a tendency to suppress or try to get rid of unpleasant feelings.

The third foundation of mindfulness is the mental formations, the activities of your mind. Observe your thoughts and feelings. Notice if you're agitated or calm, happy or depressed. Notice your despair, anger, and fear, as well as your love and compassion.

The fourth foundation of mindfulness is the objects of the mind. This has to do with your perceptions. Notice your tendency to crave and grasp at things. Notice that everything is impermanent, empty of a separate identity. Practice letting go. This brings equanimity and freedom.

At the end of the Satipatthana Sutta, the Buddha says the way to freedom is to practice the four foundations of mindfulness daily: "That is why we said that this path, the path of the four grounds for the establishment of mindfulness, is the most wonderful path, which helps beings realize purification, transcend grief and sorrow, destroy pain and anxiety, travel the right path, and realize nirvana."

To begin practicing the Four Foundations of Mindfulness, you might try the following guided meditations:

*Breathing in, I'm aware of my whole body and
I perceive all the physical sensations.
Breathing out, I'm aware of my whole body and
I calm all the physical sensations.*

*Breathing in, I listen to the arising and disappearing
of different sounds.
Breathing out, I smile at all the sounds.*

*Breathing in, I recognize physical sensations and
sounds as pleasant, unpleasant, or neutral.
Breathing out, I relax and smile at all physical
sensations and sounds.*

*Breathing in, I'm aware of my state of mind in
this moment.
Breathing out, I know this state of mind is transient
and has no substance, and I smile to my state of mind.*

*Breathing in, I'm aware that all physical and
mental formations are constantly changing.
Breathing out, I release my identification with all
physical and mental formations.*

*Breathing in, I realize that all physical and mental
formations are impermanent and have no substance.*

Breathing out, I feel free.

Breathing in, I take pleasure in my practice of mindfulness.
Breathing out, I enjoy this moment.

4

Tea Meditation

WE CAN also guide our busy minds to a peaceful state by drinking tea mindfully. We can do this on our own, with a friend, at home, or in a café. We can do it any time, even in the middle of a busy day.

First, bring awareness to the way you're sitting. Be aware of the contact of your body with the floor, your posture, how your hands are placed. Relax your body, releasing the tension in your shoulders, jaw, and all the muscles in your face. Allow your mouth to gently form a half smile. Become aware of your breath and the simple enjoyment of of sitting.

Reach for the steaming cup of tea in front of you. Feel how your hand grasps the cup. You might use both hands. Feel the warmth of the tea. Smell the tea's aroma. Completely enter the act of drinking tea.

Bring the cup to your lips and become aware of

the sensation of touch. Take one sip, hold the tea in your mouth and taste it. Feel the warmth of the tea as it goes down your throat to your stomach. As you enjoy the tea, smile.

Before you take the next sip, you might want to contemplate the origin of the tea. This cup of tea is possible because of the water that comes out of your faucet and has been transported through the pipes in your house. The water coming from those pipes flows from the big water reservoirs, where it was purified after it fell from the sky as rain or snow. Before the water was rain or snow, it was warm air that evaporated, and then it cooled and condensed into billions of tiny droplets and formed a cloud. Therefore you can say: I drink a cloud, I drink a lake, I drink the sun, and I even drink the energy of the plumber who installed the water pipes. Then, look at the tea leaves. You can see the people who created and cultivated the tea plantations in Vietnam, Japan, and India. You can see the soil that received the seeds of the tea plant, the water and the sun that allowed the plants to grow, and the people who picked the tea leaves at harvest time. Therefore, you can see the whole universe in this single cup of tea.

The following guided meditation can help you to become more fully aware of the act of drinking tea mindfully and focus your mind on the present moment:

Breathing in, I'm aware that I am sitting on a chair or cushion.
Breathing out, I enjoy sitting.

Breathing in, I'm aware of my whole body.
Breathing out, I smile to my whole body.

Breathing in, I enjoy the whole length of my in-breath.
Breathing out, I enjoy the whole length of my out-breath.

Breathing in, I'm aware of my intention of drinking tea.
Breathing out, I smile.

Breathing in, I feel how my hands hold the teacup.
Breathing out, I feel the warmth of the teacup in my hands.

Breathing in, I'm aware of how I bring the teacup to my mouth.

Breathing out, I enjoy the scent of the tea.

Breathing in, I feel the teacup touching my lips.
Breathing out, I feel and taste the tea in my mouth.

Breathing in, I feel the tea as it goes down my throat.
Breathing out, I smile at the tea as it goes down my throat toward my stomach.

Breathing in, I'm aware of all the different energies that the tea is made up of—the clouds, sun, lakes, rivers, tea plantations, soil, and tea pickers.
Breathing out, I enjoy this gift of the whole universe.

Breathing in, I enjoy my tea.
Breathing out, I smile to myself.

5

The Sun Rises Every Morning

How DID YOU wake up this morning? And how did you handle those moments of awakening? Did you say, "How wonderful, it's the beginning of a new day; I wonder what the day has in store for me. Can I embrace myself and all other beings who cross my path today with understanding, friendliness, and compassion"? Or did you say, "Oh no, yet another new day. When I start thinking about the upcoming day, it feels like way too much"?

In our unconscious minds, we have collected all different kinds of wholesome seeds of mental attitudes that may bring us happiness and joy. Of course, there are also neutral seeds and the seeds of various mental formations that bring us suffering. Which mental attitudes will manifest in our conscious minds and for how long depends on certain conditions. With mindfulness of our bodies and minds, we can affect these conditions.

Waking up in the morning, if right away you're aware of disappointments and regrets concerning the past, or if worries and fears about the future darken your spirit, it can help to make a vow to spend the day in mindfulness. Pay attention to the movement of your breath throughout the day and be willing to look at yourself and others with compassionate eyes. Throughout the day you can remind yourself to relax. This can be done with a simple smile, releasing the tension in your jaw and tongue. You can renew and strengthen your resolve to not hurt others by your actions or words. You can celebrate this intention by lighting a candle and recalling your promise for the day during your daily session of meditation. These reminders will keep you aware of your best intentions and help you to practice throughout the day.

The following guided meditation can help create the conditions for happiness as you begin each day:

Breathing in, I'm aware I'm breathing in.
Breathing out, I'm aware I'm breathing out.

Breathing in, I'm aware of the whole length of my
in-breath.

*Breathing out, I enjoy the whole length of my
out-breath.*

*Breathing in, I will do my best today to create the
conditions for more peaceful experiences.
Breathing out, I smile.*

*Breathing in, I vow to be aware of my positive traits
and regard my weaknesses with compassion.
Breathing out, I will refrain from judging myself.*

*Breathing in, I vow to see the positive traits in others
and regard their weaknesses with compassion.
Breathing out, I will refrain from judging them.*

*Breathing in, I open my heart to myself and to
others.
Breathing out, I vow that my words and actions
will be guided by kindness, compassion, and
encouragement.*

*Breathing in, I'm ready to forgive myself and others.
Breathing out, I will try to solve every conflict,
however small it may be.*

*Breathing in, I'm aware of the preciousness of
my spiritual practice.
Breathing out, I smile.*

If you can truly keep your mind focused on physical sensations by mindfully following every body movement and watching every posture, the mind won't be carried away by worry and fear. One morning when I awoke feeling sad, I experienced the power and positive effect of this practice while brushing my teeth. I'd awakened with all sorts of worries and fears that day, but I was able to focus my mind so completely on the act of brushing my teeth that my worries simply dissolved. I felt a deep peace and gratitude for the practice of simply being in the moment.

The following guided meditation will help us let go of our worries and enjoy the pure experience of being present:

Breathing in, I'm aware that I'm breathing in.
Breathing out, I'm aware that I'm breathing out.

Breathing in, I'm aware that a new day is about to begin.
Breathing out, I want to live this day in mindfulness.

Breathing in, I'm aware of my body lying on my bed.
Breathing out, I smile to my body.

*Breathing in, I'm aware of my tendency to worry
and want to make plans for the day.
Breathing out, I smile at all my plans and my
worries.*

*Breathing in, I'm aware of my feet touching the floor
as I climb out of bed.
Breathing out, I'm aware as I stand up and transfer
the weight of my body to my feet.*

*Breathing in, I'm aware of my feet carrying me to
the bathroom.
Breathing out, I'm aware of how I turn the knob to
open the bathroom door.*

*Breathing in, I see myself in the mirror.
Breathing out, I smile to myself in the mirror.*

*Breathing in, I pay attention to brushing my teeth.
Breathing out, I enjoy brushing my teeth.*

*Breathing in, I'm aware of the miracle of water
as I shower.
Breathing out, I enjoy the warm water running
over my body.*

Breathing in, I pay attention to drying myself.
Breathing out, I smile to myself.

Breathing in, I feel joy arise from my practice of
mindfulness.
Breathing out, I savor the joy in this moment.

Breathing in, I'm aware of the preciousness of my
spiritual practice.
Breathing out, I'm willing to lead a fully awakened
life.

Breathing in, I feel my breath entering my body
Breathing out, I feel my breath leaving my body

6

Bringing Joy to Others

*I vow to bring joy to one person in the morning
and to relieve the suffering of one person
in the afternoon.*
—THICH NHAT HANH[2]

THIS VOW expresses a determined readiness to comfort and encourage others with our words and deeds. We can uphold this vow by following a basic practice of performing wholesome actions. It brings me great happiness when I'm able to bring joy or comfort to a friend or a stranger. When I answer the phone and hear the voice of a friend who's suffering from a chronic illness, sometimes I have the desire to say: "I'm really sorry, I can't listen right now, because I'm a bit overwhelmed myself." Then I stop

2. Thich Nhat Hanh, "The Refuge Chant" in *Chanting From the Heart* (Berkeley, CA: Parallax Press, 2007).

and pay attention to my breath, and notice that the desire comes from old habit energy. Then, I can listen to her and maybe even say something that makes her laugh. I remind her to practice mindfulness as she prepares her breakfast and to be truly present while taking a bite of breakfast roll. The reminder to practice mindfulness during her daily tasks helps her stop the blaming and complaining that she knows doesn't do her any good. Sometimes I talk to her about my own problems, allowing her to put her problems into perspective and feel compassion for me. In this way we switch our habitual roles.

I often practice this vow when I receive a phone call from a telemarketer. I initially resent such a call since the callers are usually intrusive and pushy. Then I remind myself that the person has accepted this telemarketing job because she really needs it and couldn't find a better one. She probably faces a lot of rejection all day long. I thank her in a friendly manner and might even add, "I'm sure your work isn't easy. Have a good day!" She hasn't been able to succeed in the purpose of her call, but at least she's heard a few kind words instead of an angry response.

Another time I was able to put this vow into practice was when a repairman I've known for years came to my house with a Band-Aid on his right thumb and a protective glove on his left. I asked what happened, and he told me how stressed he was because of his schedule and the demands of his customers. I know him as a compassionate and helpful person who takes complaints to heart and tries to do right by everyone. I asked him if he would like to receive a short meditation instruction for stress reduction. I gave him some basic meditation instruction and he practiced for eight minutes. I suggested he build breaks into his workday so he could stop his rushing and thinking and could practice just being aware of his breathing during that time. He agreed and sat down on a chair in my kitchen. He was clearly pleased that I cared about his well-being, and it made me happy that I could provide him with eight minutes of stress free time on that day.

The following guided meditation can help us practice this vow to bring joy to one person in the morning and to ease the suffering of one person in the afternoon:

Breathing in, I'm aware that I'm breathing in.
Breathing out, I'm aware that I'm breathing out.

Breathing in, I want to bring joy to someone in
the morning.
Breathing out, I want to ease the suffering of
someone in the afternoon.

Breathing in, I hear the phone ringing.
Breathing out, I take three breaths and collect myself
before I pick up the phone.

Breathing in, I want to be kind to the person on
the phone.
Breathing out, I'm aware of my breathing as I listen
to what that person has to say.

Breathing in, I'm aware of the contact of my feet
with the earth or the floor.
Breathing out, I take time to find the right response.

Breathing in, I feel the suffering of the caller.
Breathing out, I find comforting, encouraging words.

Breathing in, I remember my Buddha nature,
all my positive traits resting as seeds in my store
consciousness.

Breathing out, I'm aware that I need to water these seeds daily so they can bloom.

Breathing in, I'm aware of the caller's Buddha nature.
Breathing out, I want to nourish his or her positive traits.

Breathing in, I'm aware that my spiritual practice is precious.
Breathing out, I smile to myself and to all beings that make it possible for me to practice.

7
Letting Go

THERE ARE MANY wonderful opportunities in life to practice letting go. One opportunity is going on vacation. People like to travel because they long to leave their everyday worries, fears, and problems behind for a while. Leaving your familiar surroundings with all their comforts forces you to increase your awareness as you adjust to a new environment. This is sometimes enough of a change to let go of your everyday troubles.

Breathing and walking meditation are also wonderful opportunities to practice letting go. You need to let go of your in-breath in order to fully experience your out-breath. And you need to let go of your out-breath in order to fully experience the next in-breath. You need to complete the step with the left leg in order to step with the right leg.

As you become more aware and able to let go of

small things in your life, it will eventually become easier to let go of the more significant things, such as the suffering that comes with the loss of a loved one, a job, a relationship; having to leave your country for political or economic reasons; or losing your health as you become chronically ill or grow older and more fragile.

You can ask yourself, "Can I truly open myself up to all the changes in this new situation?" This can help you develop acceptance, equanimity, and curiosity. Once in an obituary I read a quote from the Sufi master Hazrat Inayat Khan. It has accompanied me ever since: "When the roof over your head collapses, you can finally see the sky." This quote continues to help me let go and develop an unconditional acceptance toward what is and what will be. Practicing with the small things helped me to see that I'm increasing my ability to rediscover the sky during the difficult times as well.

Here is an example of practicing with a small irritation. I arrived at a nice meditation center for a weekend seminar. We could choose between double rooms and dorm rooms. Upon my arrival, I chose a double room, looking forward to sharing it with Annette, who was my roommate for a whole month during a trip to Vietnam. Annette would arrive a day later, but I was looking forward to intimate conversations with her during breaks and in the evening before we retired.

After breakfast, a woman came up to me and told me very happily that her name was Beatrice and that she had just moved from a dorm room into my room because she hadn't found the dorm room to her liking.

I said, "I already have a roommate, my friend Annette. She'll arrive this afternoon. We've been planning to share the room."

"But I've already moved my things in." said Beatrice.

I said, "I understand. But Annette will be here shortly and we have both been looking forward to sharing a room." Beatrice didn't respond. At that point I gave in. I didn't want to hurt her and it wasn't necessary to be too attached to my preference. "All right," I said, "then let's leave it the way it is."

I was aware of my practice of letting go and I asked myself, "Am I willing to be at ease with this situation and let go of my expectations?" When Annette arrived, I described the situation to her and she moved into the dorm room without further comment. She's a good practitioner of letting go. I was aware that I needed to open my heart toward Beatrice for us to be at ease and have a good time together. And, as it turned out, we had a lot to say to each other. It ended up being a friendly and interesting experience because I was able to let go of my irritation and disappointment.

The following guided meditation can help you to let go of expectations and be open to change:

Breathing in, I'm aware that I'm breathing in.
Breathing out, I'm aware that I'm breathing out.

Breathing in, I know I must let go of my in-breath so my out-breath can follow.
Breathing out, I know I must let go of my out-breath so my in-breath can follow.

Breathing in, I know I have completed this step.
Breathing out, I know I have completed this next step.

Breathing in, I am aware that I'm opening the door.
Breathing out, I am aware that I'm closing the door.

Breathing in, looking forward to my vacation, I smile.
Breathing out, knowing I need to let go of my

familiar surroundings, I smile.

*Breathing in, I notice that someone's behavior
doesn't agree with my expectations.
Breathing out, I take a deep look to discern what I
need to let go of.*

*Breathing in, I'm aware that I need to leave my
house, my city, or my country.
Breathing out, I am mindful of every step.*

*Breathing in, I read the letter announcing the
termination of my employment.
Breathing out, I gently give myself a hug and I'm
willing to let go.*

*Breathing in, I hear the words of someone very dear
who tells me that he or she wants to leave me.
Breathing out, I gently give myself a hug and I am
willing to let him or her go.
I will keep my heart open for other people.*

*Breathing in, I let all worries, problems, and plans
drift by like clouds in a windy sky.
Breathing out, I smile at the clouds on a windy day.*

8

Developing Stability, Ease, and Freedom

IT's IMPORTANT to practice mindfulness during "normal times," when we're doing well so we'll be able to practice in difficult times. Mindful breathing, mindful walking, and mindfulness in daily activities nourish energies in us that allow stability, lightness, equanimity, and joy to arise. If we familiarize ourselves with basic mindfulness practices bringing peace to our minds during "normal times," then we'll be able to rely on these practices when we experience strong, upsetting emotions.

All mental formations—whether wholesome, unwholesome, or neutral—begin as seeds in our store consciousness. They manifest in mind consciousness when conditions allow them to be touched off. It's important to recognize difficult mental formations and become conscious of them as they arise. It doesn't help to say to oneself, "I'm not really angry," or "I'm not disappointed," or "I'm not desperate." To have the attitude of repressing difficult emotions is the result of ignorance. Ignorance is one of the three "poisons" in Buddhism, along with greed and hate. It's important to recognize despair, anger, disappointment, and other emotions as they arise.

The Buddha said that a person who refuses to recognize his or her own suffering is like a mule walking around with a heavy load, unable to get rid of it. I laugh when I think of this example, especially when I catch myself acting like the mule. It's helpful to ask myself in that moment, "Are you aware that you're suffering? Are you willing to let go of the burden that causes you so much pain?" Phrasing it as a question allows me to be mindful of my mental formation. I begin to identify less with the difficult emotion and create space for deeper exploration and understanding of my situation.

Once I'm more aware of what's occurring in the moment, I can begin to become aware of my breathing and of the physical sensations in my body as I observe my in-breath and out-breath. I'm able to observe more closely how the difficult feeling is being expressed.

When I'm afraid or upset, my throat feels tight and my hands are clammy. When I feel anger or rage, I get hot and feel as though I might explode. When I experience despair or depression, my whole body feels weak. When I'm able to completely focus my mind on the movement of my breath, it takes only a few minutes to restore some stability and freshness in my body and mind. If, in these moments, I can remember to embrace the difficult mental formations with compassion, kindness, and patience, then I feel safe.

If I'm able to ask myself, "Is it possible for me to encounter this anger, despair, or depression with compassion and embrace it with great tenderness?" then I can guide my mind in a new direction and create the space necessary for transforming the difficult feeling. I find that using the form of a question is important. Asking a question isn't meant to create additional stress or to suggest that I shouldn't feel anger or fear; instead it should create openness and help me become aware that mindfulness, patience, and compassion will give me the freedom not to surrender to negative feelings. This kind of internal questioning helps me to stop repeating the story that brought up these feelings in the first place.

When I commit myself to a regular practice of dealing with my difficult mental formations, I notice that they lose their strength; they return to my store consciousness a little bit weaker. Over the years, I've noticed that habitual patterns of thinking that cause me to suffer have begun to gradually dissolve in my store consciousness. I started to recognize the old story that had led to the painful feeling, and I was able to change the story. This is a wonderful exercise. At a certain point the practice of changing the story and transforming the difficult feelings started to be fun. Right in the middle of a difficult feeling of impatience, anger, irritation, or despair, the winds turned and the feeling whispered, "Don't be afraid; all you need to do is embrace me."

The fear of difficult emotions is an incredibly strong force that pushes us to immediately suppress our difficult feelings. But when those feelings are suppressed, they can't heal. Sometimes we harbor the fear that we won't be loved if others notice that we have these negative feelings, so we repress them. But as we gradually accept and lose our fear of the difficult emotions, we stop worrying about being overwhelmed or dominated by them.

PARALLAX
PRESS

Please send in this card to receive a copy of our catalog.
Add your email address to sign up for our monthly newsletter.

Please print

Name _____

Address _____

City _____ State _____ Zip _____

Country _____

Email _____

facebook.com/parallaxpress • parallax.org • twitter.com/parallaxpress

Get the latest news, author updates, and special offers online!

PARALLAX PRESS

P.O. Box 7355

Berkeley, CA 94707

Becoming aware of difficult feelings in a nonjudgmental way allows you to acknowledge them when they arise without being overwhelmed by them. If you can embrace them, just as a mother embraces her crying child, then the fear will disappear. Doing this means taking a leap forward in your practice; this can change your whole life. If you really wish to dissolve the tight pain in your heart, you have no choice but to keep practicing on your own and with others. Your practice will not only help yourself, but it will also have a positive influence on the people who share your life.

The following guided meditation can help you to develop stability and calmness when you face difficult emotions. It can also help you pass on this positive energy to your environment.

Breathing in, I'm aware that I am breathing in.
Breathing out, I'm aware that I am breathing out.

With every conscious breath, my mind and my body
receive freshness and ease.
As I breathe out, I transmit freshness and ease
to my environment.

*With every conscious breath I receive stability
and peace.
As I breathe out, I transmit stability and peace to
my environment.*

*Every conscious breath brings me equanimity.
Breathing out, I transmit equanimity to
my environment.*

*Every conscious breath helps me develop
concentration.
Breathing out, I transmit the joy of concentration
to my environment.*

*Every conscious breath helps me acknowledge,
embrace, and transform my disappointment.
Breathing out, I transmit this freedom to
my environment.*

*Every conscious breath helps me acknowledge,
embrace, and transform my anger. Breathing out,
I transmit this freedom to my environment.*

*Every conscious breath helps me acknowledge,
embrace, and transform my despair.
Breathing out, I transmit this freedom to
my environment.*

*Every conscious breath helps me to acknowledge,
embrace, and transform my fear. Breathing out, I
transmit this freedom to my environment.*

*Every conscious breath helps me to better
understand myself and other beings.
Breathing out, I can help ease the suffering of others.*

*Breathing in, I enjoy the preciousness of my
spiritual practice.
Breathing out, I smile.*

9

Mindfulness in Everyday Life

THE PRACTICE OF MINDFULNESS is the heart of Buddhist meditation. Mindfulness is the ability to be in touch with what's going on in our bodies and minds in that very moment. Each moment we spend in mindfulness lifts the fog of the judgmental, grasping mind from our spiritual vision. Mindfulness is like a mirror reflecting what is; nothing is distorted.

The Buddhist teacher Ruth Denison says, "Mindfulness doesn't grasp at anything. It doesn't deny or add anything. It doesn't attract nor reject. It's pure presence, and it's a presence that's possible in every single moment of our life."

Even with the many tasks we need to get done in daily life, mindfulness is possible. We don't need a god or guru to guide us; mindfulness is within us. Mindfulness allows us to have an unbiased perspective. As we look at the world with curious amazement, we are filled with freshness, vigor, and lightness of being. Our life becomes much more interesting because we're no longer judging and categorizing everything we encounter. Our view of ourselves, of others, of our situations, and our encounters shifts when we're mindful. The true nature of ourselves, of others, or of a situation is revealed and we start to communicate in a different way.

When you practice mindfulness, you start to become the witness of your life. Being fully present, you no longer feel separate but are aware of your connection with everything that is. Whether your experiences are joyful or difficult, you can maintain a deep inner calm and peace. As you observe what's happening in your body and mind, you have more clarity to see which of your qualities to cultivate and which to let go of in order to create more joy and less suffering within yourself.

The following guided meditation can help you to develop mindfulness in your everyday life. You can choose the phrases appropriate to the activity you're engaged in, or you can make up your own:

Breathing in, I feel my breath entering my body.
Breathing out, I feel my breath leaving my body.

Breathing in, I'm aware that I'm wiping the kitchen
table clean.
Breathing out, I smile to myself.

Breathing in, I'm aware that I'm setting the table.
Breathing out, I enjoy my movements as I set
the table.

Breathing in, I'm aware that I'm cleaning the toilet.
Breathing out, I smile as I clean the toilet.

Breathing in, I'm aware that I feel bored.
Breathing out, I smile at the feeling of boredom.

Breathing in, I feel fear arising in me.
Breathing out, I smile at the feeling of fear.

Breathing in, I hear a door close in the house.
Breathing out, I smile.

Breathing in, I listen to a dog barking.
Breathing out, I smile.

Breathing in, I'm aware of the preciousness of my spiritual practice.
Breathing out, I realize it can bring me peace and healing in every moment of my life.

10

Gratitude, Joy, and Compassion

ONE OF OUR MOST popular activities has become the acquisition of things. In our consumer society, feelings of depression, meaninglessness, and despair are widespread. These feelings can be a reflection of what's missing in our society. We often lack gratitude for all the things, material and immaterial, available to us. Changing our perspective, so that we enjoy and focus on what we already have, we feel better. This enables us to have more compassion and understanding for those who have less than we do. Usually we only become aware of our good fortune when there's a threat of losing it due to illness, old age, death, or conflict.

Once when I was shopping I met an older, overweight lady using a walker. She had a difficult time moving forward and did so very slowly. I noticed she was really interested in my dachshund. I stopped so she could greet and pet him. We started talking and she told me that for the past ten years she had been taking care of her husband who had lost both his legs. She often had to lift him and so had suffered a herniated disc.

We parted in a friendly manner, and as I turned around one more time to wave goodbye, I saw that she was showing interest in the next dog that had come along with its owner. In that moment, I felt full of admiration for the inner strength she showed in mastering her life. Our meeting had enriched me. I felt gratitude for our encounter as well as for the fact that I could still walk well. I have mild sciatica, but I don't have a damaged spine.

Developing gratitude, joy, and compassion can be the best medicine to counteract feelings of depression, meaninglessness, and despair. You can access this medicine daily by acknowledging the many treasures you have in the present moment.

The following guided meditation can help you to develop gratitude, joy, and compassion to transform difficult emotions such as futility and despair.

Breathing in, I'm aware that I'm breathing in.
Breathing out, I'm aware that I'm breathing out.

Breathing in, I feel the full length of my in-breath.
Breathing out, I enjoy the full length of my
out-breath.

Breathing in, I know I'm fortunate to be able to sleep
in a sheltered room tonight.
Breathing out, I wish that all beings may be
protected and safe tonight.

Breathing in, I'm happy and grateful that I have
enough to eat.
Breathing out, I will work so that all beings will
have enough to eat.

Breathing in, I'm happy and grateful to be able to
walk, stand, and run.
Breathing out, I embrace all beings who aren't able
to walk, stand, or run.

Breathing in, I'm happy that I can calm and
refresh my mind by practicing walking and sitting
meditation.
Breathing out, I smile to all my spiritual teachers
with gratitude.

Breathing in, I'm happy that I know my
mindfulness and compassion can heal negative
mental formations.
Breathing out, I want to share this practice
with others.

Breathing in, I enjoy the healing power of nature.
Breathing out, I thank all the trees, bushes, flowers,
and rivers for their existence.

Breathing in, I am aware of the preciousness of my
spiritual practice.
Breathing out, I smile.

11

Six Wonderful Realizations

IN BUDDHISM, there are six wonderful mental formations called the *paramitas*, or perfections. Cultivating the paramitas through our practice of mindfulness and gratitude, we gradually dissolve our hindrances and the despair they bring. The six wonderful mental formations are *dana*—generosity, giving; *shila*—morality, ethics; *kshanti*—patience, inclusiveness; *virya*—enthusiastic perseverance, vigor; *dhyana*—meditation, concentration; *prajña*—understanding, wisdom, insight. When we look deeply into each paramita we see that it contains the other five.

You might choose one paramita to practice. If you want to practice the paramita of generosity, you can look ahead at your day and see who you'll be meeting and what situations you'll be in that will allow you to practice generosity. You can show generosity in both material and nonmaterial ways. Practicing generosity not only benefits others, but it also benefits oneself greatly. You have many possible ways to express your generosity. Someone might need to be listened to and may benefit from your stability, impartiality, and good judgment. If someone is taking things too seriously, he or she may benefit from your cheerfulness. You could offer to go grocery shopping for a sick neighbor, baby-sit children or grandchildren for a friend, or work for a relief organization.

The Chinese translation of paramita means "to cross over to the other shore." This means that we go from the shore of suffering to the shore of well-being. We can ask ourselves, "What is the other shore in my situation, and what will help me get there?"

The practice of mindfulness, concentration, and insight gives you the opportunity to recognize when you're stranded on the shore of despair, fear, disappointment, loneliness, or jealousy. By embracing your difficult feelings with mindfulness and compassion, you allow them to dissolve, and you can cross over to the other shore of freedom. Freeing yourself from these difficult feelings is a great gift to yourself and to your environment.

If you were to express this as an intention, you

might say: "I would like to develop freshness, stability, peace, calm, and equanimity, and I'll pass on these wonderful attributes of the spirit to the people around me. These attributes will find expression in my whole being, in my speech, and in my behavior."

One of the practices that touched me the most when I was in Plum Village was the practice of walking hand in hand with someone you don't know during walking meditation. At first, I was just watching others do this and I felt too shy to do it myself. I felt a subtle tinge of loneliness when I saw how many people were taking part in this practice. I was used to the silent retreats of the vipassana tradition of Theravada Buddhism, in which we received instructions to avoid eye contact. Physical contact was even less of an option. Given my background, the practice of walking hand in hand and communicating with others in this direct way was new and seemed very special and unique.

At one of the long summer retreats in Plum Village, I'd spoken publicly about spending time with my mother during the last few months of her life. A nun who felt touched by my story came over to me at the start of walking meditation. She bowed and took my hand. She did it in such a clear and straightforward way that I felt very happy as we walked together with Thich Nhat Hanh and the Sangha around the lotus pond. I hardly knew her; there had even been a minor incident earlier when I caught myself judging her because she had behaved in a way that I didn't approve of. Now she had come to me, had taken my hand, and we were walking together as if we were best friends. To simply feel her warm hand and to settle into every step taken together very mindfully was enough to let go of any prejudice I might have harbored against her.

The clarity and solidity the nun expressed as she bowed and took my hand taught me a lot. It showed me how easy it can be to let go of shyness and feelings of loneliness. Since that experience, I've often invited others to walk hand in hand with me during walking meditation. It has helped me to conquer my shyness.

The following guided meditation can help develop the six paramitas.

Breathing in, I know I'm breathing in.
Breathing out, I know I'm breathing out.

Breathing in, I want to cultivate my generosity.
Breathing out, I want to share my time, energy,

knowledge, and material possessions with those around me.

Breathing in, I'm ready to open my heart and feel compassion for my own weaknesses and the weaknesses of others.
Breathing out, I to myself and others.

Breathing in, I vow to practice to transform my negative habit energies and cultivate healing energies.
Breathing out, I vow to share the fruits of my perseverance and stability with others.

Breathing in, I will keep coming back to my breath to develop concentration and calmness.
Breathing out, I will share my concentration and calmness with those around me.

Breathing in, I vow to develop deep understanding and insight.
Breathing out, I'm aware of my connection with other people, animals, and plants.

Breathing in, I'm aware of my whole body.
Breathing out, I smile to my whole body.

The following guided meditation can specifically help develop the *kshanti* paramita, opening the heart and including everyone:

> *Breathing in, I'm aware that I'm breathing in.*
> *Breathing out, I'm aware that I'm breathing out.*
>
> *Breathing in, I open my heart wide and acknowledge my weaknesses.*
> *Breathing out, I embrace my difficult habit energies with compassion.*
>
> *Breathing in, I'm aware of my own positive character traits without feeling pride in them.*
> *Breathing out, I'm full of joy.*
>
> *Breathing in, I open my heart wide and recognize the weaknesses of a dear friend.*
> *Breathing out, I embrace my friend's difficult habit energies with compassion.*
>
> *Breathing in, I'm aware of the positive character traits of a dear friend.*
> *Breathing out, I'm full of joy.*
>
> *Breathing in, I open my heart to the difficult habit energies of someone who is neutral to me.*

*Breathing out, I meet this neutral person
with compassion.*

*Breathing in, I become aware of the positive traits
of someone who is neutral to me.
Breathing out, I'm full of joy.*

*Breathing in, I open my heart to the negative habit
energies of a person I'm experiencing difficulty with.
Breathing out, I feel compassion for this person.*

*Breathing in, I become aware of the positive traits of
someone I'm experiencing difficulty with.
Breathing out, I'm full of joy.*

*Breathing in, I'm aware that everyone carries
wholesome and unwholesome seeds in their
store consciousness.
Breathing out, I want to water the wholesome seeds
in others and observe their unwholesome seeds
with compassion.*

*Breathing in, I'm aware of the preciousness of my
spiritual practice.
Breathing out, I smile.*

12

The Four Immeasurable Minds

THE FOUR IMMEASURABLE MINDS are also known as the Four *Brahmaviharas*, or the Four Aspects of Love. These states of mind arise through the practice of mindfulness, concentration, and insight. We may also cultivate them deliberately by inviting them into our consciousness by using certain phrases to guide our formal meditation practice.

The first immeasurable mind is *metta*, loving kindness, caring for all beings. Developing loving kindness means making an effort to welcome all beings with an open heart. In the Metta Sutta, the Buddha teaches that we should look upon all beings as if we were their mother. A mother provides the best care for her child and does everything possible to further that child's well-being. Mental states such as anger, wrath, and clinging are the opposite of kindness. These states inevitably lead to suffering. For example, clinging could manifest in a relationship in which one partner doesn't allow the other space and acts in a controlling way.

The second immeasurable mind is *karuna*, compassion for the suffering of other beings. This state is about doing everything possible to alleviate the physical and mental suffering of others. The opposite mental states of compassion are cruelty, wishing to inflict harm on others, or pity. Pity, for example, causes us to feel superior to others.

The third immeasurable mind is *mudita*, joy. Joy arises as we practice love and compassion, but it also arises by simply being in touch with the small and large miracles in our lives. We can share our joy with others, and we can join in their joy as well. Sympathetic or shared joy is an effective remedy for envy and jealousy, which we often feel when others are successful. It's important to embrace our envy and jealousy with a lot of compassion for those states to dissipate; only then can we experience shared joy. The opposite mental state of shared joy is jealousy. When we praise and acknowledge others in a dishonest way, our motivation may be to manipulate them according to our own desires.

The fourth immeasurable state of mind is *upeksha*, equanimity, a balanced, unbiased, and nonjudgmental state of mind. Upeksha means that we're open and don't take sides. We try to understand and empathize with both perspectives. Equanimity is not the same as indifference, which is aversion and manifests as an apathetic attitude.

The four Brahmaviharas are interconnected and support each other. Equanimity, for example, helps us to avoid becoming possessive in a close relationship and allows space for both partners to feel free. It can also mean that we remain loving, compassionate, and kind toward people who hurt us, because we see that they are acting out of ignorance.

The following guided meditation helps us cultivate loving kindness, compassion, joy, and equanimity.

Breathing in, I know that I'm breathing in.
Breathing out, I know that I'm breathing out.

Breathing in, I welcome myself with an open heart.
Breathing out, I welcome others with an open heart.

Breathing in, I'm willing to embrace my physical
and mental pain with compassion.

Breathing out, I'm willing to embrace the pain of others with compassion.

Breathing in, I will water the seeds of joy and happiness within me every day.
Breathing out, I will water the seeds of joy and happiness in others every day.

Breathing in, I will recognize clinging and aversion in myself.
Breathing out, I will let go of clinging and aversion.

Breathing in, I will look on all beings with acceptance, love, and understanding.
Breathing out, I will give others their freedom without slipping into indifference.

Breathing in, I will live refreshed, solidly, and freely.
Breathing out, I will nourish freshness, solidity, and freedom in others.

Breathing in, I am aware of the preciousness of my spiritual practice.
Breathing out, I smile.

13

Loving Kindness Meditation

L OVING KINDNESS meditation is a very special practice that allows us to transform fear, anger, vindictiveness, and other negative emotions we may harbor toward other living beings. It is a powerful practice that helps practitioners develop an all-encompassing kindness toward all beings. We need inner peace, stability, and open hearts to develop deep understanding and unconditional love. This is a never-ending practice that helps us feel connected to all life, including animals, plants, and minerals.

Rosa Luxemburg, a well-known socialist who lived at the beginning of the twentieth century, writes in *Letters from Prison* about how she appreciates the different animals that visit her cell: a butterfly, a bird, or an ant crawling on the window sill. She writes, "Before noon I found a peacock butterfly in the bathroom window. It must have been inside for a few days...its wings gave only weak signs of life. As I noticed it, I climbed up to the window and picked it up carefully with my hands. It didn't fight at all, and I thought it might be dead. I put it down on the window ledge. It didn't move. Then I put a few flowers right in front of its antennae, thinking it might want to eat. After half an hour the tiny animal recovered. It began moving around a bit, and then slowly flew off. How I rejoiced in the success of this rescue mission!"

When you do metta meditation, you always begin with yourself. You develop the capacity to embrace yourself with understanding and love. Then you extend this love to a friend or family member. It's best not to begin the practice with someone you're having difficulty with or someone you're too passionate about. Then, you practice extending this love to a neutral person, then to a difficult person and, at the end of the practice, you extend your love and understanding to all beings.

The following guided meditation helps to develop loving kindness toward yourself and other beings.

Breathing in, I feel my breath entering my body.
Breathing out, I feel my breath leaving my body.

Breathing in, I look on myself with understanding
and love.
Breathing out, I look on myself with understanding
and love.

Breathing in, I look on a close friend with
understanding and love.
Breathing out, I look on a close friend with
understanding and love.

Breathing in, I look on a neutral person with
understanding and love.
Breathing out, I look on a neutral person with
understanding and love.

Breathing in, I look on a difficult person with
understanding and love.
Breathing out, I look on a difficult person with
understanding and love.

Breathing in, I look on the one I love with
understanding and compassion.
Breathing out, I look on the one I love with
understanding and compassion.

Breathing in, I aspire to regard everyone in my community with understanding and love.
Breathing out, I am open myself to regard everyone in my community with understanding and love.

Breathing in, I am willing to regard everyone who rides the bus or subway with me with understanding and love.
Breathing out, I am willing to regard everyone who rides the bus or subway with me with understanding and love.

Breathing in, I am willing to regard all beings with understanding and love.
Breathing out, I am willing to regard all beings with understanding and love.

Breathing in, I am aware of the preciousness of my spiritual practice.
Breathing out, I smile.

The following is an additional guided *metta* meditation:

May I be peaceful, happy, and at ease in body and spirit.
May all beings be peaceful, happy, and at ease in body and spirit.

May I be safe and protected.
May all beings be safe and protected.

May I learn to regard myself with understanding and love.
May I learn to regard all beings with understanding and love.

May I nourish the seeds of joy in myself every day.
May I nourish the seeds of joy in all beings every day.

May I be fresh, solid, and free.
May all beings be fresh, solid, and free.

14

Feeling the World's Joy and Pain

IT'S A BRIGHT and sunny May morning in Berlin. Flowers and leaves are springing up everywhere. Light and shade alternate on the sidewalk. I'm on my way into the city to see my homeopathic doctor. Then I plan to stroll over to the Wednesday market at Hohenzollernplatz.

As I pass 61 Nassauische Strasse I notice nineteen golden paving stones glowing in the sun. I know these stones. A few years ago I sponsored several of them to be engraved and placed on sidewalks in my own city district. The stones are part of a monument called *Stolpersteine*, stumbling stones, created by Gunter Demnig, which commemorates victims and survivors of the Holocaust. I read the names: Margarete and Siegfried Levy, deported to Auschwitz on April 19, 1943, killed in Auschwitz; Marianne Klatt, committed suicide before deportation; Amalie Sorauer, deported to Theresienstadt in 1942, killed in 1943; Georg and Max Blumenfeld, deported to Sobibor and Treblinka in 1942, killed in Treblinka; Margarete Stern, deported and killed in Theresienstadt in 1942.

I imagine these people's fear and desperation, and the panic they probably felt when they were arrested. I imagine the stench in the trains they were transported in and how tightly packed they were in there. I feel the agony they must have felt living in the camp quarters at Auschwitz—the cold, the hunger, and finally suffocating in the gas chambers.

I open the door to my car, stow away my shopping bags, and sit down next to my small dachshund. I pet him and enjoy his liveliness.

Buddhism says that consciousness doesn't only exist on an individual level, but also collectively. I feel a deep pain that this violence happened right here in my country, but I'm greatly relieved that it's a different country today. I'm happy to have this tiny glimpse of freedom. It represents that transformation is possible, individually and collectively.

When we detect physical or mental pain and weakness in ourselves and in others, we often react with defensiveness and resistance, which only increases and intensifies the pain. When we encounter suffering with openness in an accepting and compassionate way, the pain may dissolve, and it's almost guaranteed that it won't increase. Joanna Macy, a scholar of Buddhism and deep ecology, once said, "Our heart must break again and again, until it's free."

If you learn to deal with your own physical and mental pain compassionately and embrace your suffering with love, it will be easier for you to embrace the pain of other beings with compassion. When you come into contact with your inner abundance, your energy flows out into the world. When you experience your connection to the universe and no longer feel isolated and separate, you often don't experience as much pain and suffering. Feelings of depression, fear, panic, or purposelessness can fade away or arise less frequently. Stephen Levine, a spiritual teacher who worked with the dying and chronically ill, put it this way: "The deepest healing can never take place in separation. It has to contribute to the whole, to the pain that we all share. Seeing that it's not simply my pain, but *the* pain, the circle of healing expands to allow the universe to enter."

There's so much suffering in the world. We often

feel like there's nothing of significance we can do to help the people and animals in these situations. But you can always send compassion to all beings that are suffering. You can open your heart wide to include all suffering beings. When your compassion finds expression in your actions and is based on deep understanding, it's no longer simply theoretical. You can then live your life fully and find joy in all your encounters with other beings.

The following guided meditation can help you to open up to your own pain and the pain of the world and embrace the pain with compassion:

Breathing in, I feel the air entering my body.
Breathing out, I feel the air leaving my body.

Breathing in, I feel my tenderness for all life.
Breathing out, I smile.

Breathing in, I inhale the freshness all around me.
Breathing out, I feel that freshness within me.

Breathing in, I want to do whatever I can to protect myself, others, and the environment.
Breathing out, I smile.

Breathing in, I embrace my physical and emotional pain and weaknesses with compassion.
Breathing out, my compassion grows.

Breathing in, I encounter the physical and emotional pain and weaknesses of a dear friend with compassion.
Breathing out, my compassion grows.

Breathing in, I will encounter a neutral person with compassion.
Breathing out, my compassion grows.

Breathing in, I will encounter the physical and emotional pains of a difficult person with compassion.
Breathing out, my compassion grows.

Breathing in, I will encounter the physical and emotional pain of someone I love/the one I love with compassion.
Breathing out, my compassion grows.

Breathing in, I vow to look with the eyes of compassion at the physical and emotional pain of those around me.

*Breathing out, I look with the eyes of compassion at
the physical and emotional pain of those around me.*

*Breathing in, I am willing to encounter the physical
and emotional pain and weaknesses of all beings
with compassion.*
Breathing out, my compassion grows.

Breathing in, I open my heart to my own pain.
*Breathing out, I open my heart to the pain of
the world.*

Breathing in, I feel how I breathe in.
Breathing out, I feel how I breathe out.

15

Nourishing Happiness

WISHING OURSELVES and others well reminds us to identify, touch, and nourish the seeds of joy and happiness within. Our goal is to recognize these positive seeds daily.

This can be difficult for many of us. It helps to keep in mind that the way we perceive the world is often very limited. Our habit energies compel our minds again and again to dwell on painful emotions like inferiority, despair, anger, jealousy, worries, and depression, rather than the joys in our life. We often forget that Buddha nature is always present inside us.

The essence of this practice is to constantly be willing to remember the qualities of the awakened spirit, and to realize that everyone carries the seeds of joy and happiness in his or her store consciousness. It's important to remember that it's possible to touch these seeds at any time and allow them to blossom.

We can decide to focus on the joyful things in our lives, such as the sun warming our faces in springtime, the gentle touch of a ladybug, the good food a friend has prepared, the sound of raindrops, the roaring of the wind in the fall, the stillness of a winter night, the joy of playing with friends, children, and animals, or the delight in finding a meaningful item long thought lost.

We can also call to mind the joys that result directly from our spiritual practice. We feel joy when we are calm, concentrated, and clear because we have repeatedly guided the mind back to the awareness of the breath. We can recall the joy that arises when we're able to transform difficult feelings, judgmental words, or unwholesome deeds. We can rejoice at being able to let go of our limited perception of others. Our spiritual practice might also give rise to certain insights that bring us joy.

The more you cultivate your Buddha nature, the more joy and happiness you'll be able to manifest in your life. You'll be able to fully realize and experience the positive qualities in yourself and the positive aspects of the situations you encounter.

On some days you might want to practice with

phrases that focus on nourishing and supporting yourself. On other days you might practice with phrases
that extend that support to other beings. The wonderful quality of the words will eventually penetrate
every cell in your body and allow you to develop trust
in this practice.

The following guided meditation can help you to
recognize and nourish the seeds of joy and happiness
in yourself and all beings:

> *Breathing in, I'm aware that I'm breathing in.*
> *Breathing out, I'm aware that I'm breathing out.*
>
> *Breathing in, I will recognize the seeds of joy and*
> *happiness in myself every day.*
> *Breathing out, I will recognize the seeds of joy and*
> *happiness in myself every day.*
>
> *Breathing in, I recognize and nourish the seeds of joy*
> *and happiness in a dear friend.*
> *Breathing out, I recognize and nourish the seeds of*
> *joy and happiness in a dear friend.*
>
> *Breathing in, I recognize and nourish the seeds of joy*
> *and happiness in a neutral person.*

Breathing out, I recognize and nourish the seeds of joy and happiness in a neutral person.

Breathing in, I recognize and nourish the seeds of joy and happiness in a difficult person.
Breathing out, I recognize and nourish the seeds of joy and happiness in a difficult person.

Breathing in, I recognize and nourish the seeds of joy and happiness in my loved one. Breathing out, I recognize and nourish the seeds of joy and happiness in my loved one.

Breathing in, I want to recognize and nourish the seeds of joy and happiness in all sentient beings. Breathing out, I want to recognize and nourish the seeds of joy and happiness in all sentient beings.

Breathing in, I am aware of the preciousness of my spiritual practice.
Breathing out, I smile.

16

Love and Compassion for Animals

BY PRACTICING MINDFULNESS, loving kindness, and compassion we feel more deeply connected with all living beings. At the same time we begin to understand on a deeper level that it's essential for our own protection and well-being to take care of our environment. We begin to understand that we don't exist separately from animals and our natural surroundings. Thich Nhat Hanh says, "Looking deeply into the human species, we can recognize the non-human elements. And when we look deeply into the species of animals, plants, and minerals we discover the human elements within them. When we become aware of the signless nature of external appearances, we will live in harmony with all species."[3]

3. Thich Nhat Hanh, *The Heart of the Buddha's Teaching* (New York: Broadway Books, 1999)

The Buddha gave us five ethical principles, which Thich Nhat Hanh has adapted for our time as the Five Mindfulness Trainings, to guide us in acting mindfully toward other living beings. They express a commitment to abstain from harming living beings, stealing, sexual misconduct, untruthful speech, and intoxication. The first precept that states we should neither kill nor hurt a living being also applies to animals. We can pick snails off of the leaves of flowers or a zucchini plant and set them free elsewhere. If bees and flies are trapped inside the house, we can let them out. We can pick up spiders carefully and carry them outside, and so on.

Once we start to practice these principals of non-harming, we may want to reduce our consumption of meat and fish, since we know that it causes suffering for animals. We might start eating vegetarian or vegan. A reduction in, or abstinence from, eating meat or animal products can strengthen the connection we feel with all of life and bring a feeling of comfort.

The following guided meditation can help us to develop love and compassion for animals.

Breathing in, I'm aware I'm breathing in.
Breathing out, I'm aware I'm breathing out.

Breathing in, I feel the gentle touch of a fly crawling on my hand.
Breathing out, I smile at the fly.

Breathing in, I see a desperate bee circling around my kitchen window.
Breathing out, I open the window and set the bee free.

Breathing in, I pick the snails from my flowers and lettuce and take them outside the garden.
Breathing out, I wish them a good new beginning.

Breathing in, I picture cows and their calves peacefully grazing in summer meadows.
Breathing out, I want to reduce my consumption of meat or become vegetarian or vegan to save the cows from being slaughtered.

Breathing in, I watch fish dart through the water in the lake or stream.
Breathing out, I enjoy their energy.

Breathing in, I listen to crickets chirp on a warm summer night.
Breathing out, I enjoy their evening concert.

Breathing in, I'm aware I'm breathing in.
Breathing out, I smile to all my animal friends.

17

The Five Powers

THE BUDDHA SPOKE of Five Powers that each of us can develop: trust, perseverance, mindfulness, concentration, and insight, or deep understanding. When we commit ourselves to nurturing these five spiritual strengths (*indriya*), they begin to unfold in our whole being.

All five of these spiritual faculties are connected to each other, and each faculty supports the development of the others. Faith is needed in order to begin a spiritual practice. You need perseverance in order to evolve in your practice, transform suffering, and recognize the elements that enhance our happiness and well-being. Mindfulness is required to become aware of what's happening within you and in your surroundings. When you're mindful, you're more able to see what causes your own suffering and that of others. You're also more able to notice what advances well-being. When mindfulness is developed by practicing walking and sitting meditation in our daily life on a continuing basis, the mind will be able to concentrate more and more. Concentration shouldn't be forced, but it should be a steady effort to be in contact with the experience of the present moment. You can experience this concentration every time you mindfully wash the dishes, clean, sweep, cut vegetables, and so on. The practice of concentration can bring a steady calmness to your daily life. From this inner calm, a deep understanding about your life may develop. You need a certain depth of understanding to keep your faith in your spiritual practice alive. One aspect of this understanding is the insight that your true happiness doesn't depend on any specific pleasant sensation because all sensations are fleeting.

I remember a moment when I was able to appreciate the fruits of developing these five spiritual faculties. On the last day of a retreat at Dhamma Dena, Ruth Denison's spiritual center in the Mojave Desert, I intended to enjoy walking and sitting meditation peacefully at the center. But my teacher Ruth had a different idea. She said, "Annabelle, I need to go to Palm Springs, why don't you come with me?" I didn't really feel like going, because every trip to the city involved running many errands and stopping at lots of shops. But I said yes since I always like spending time with Ruth. At first we stopped at a gas station because the car needed a minor repair. This was the last sort of activity I would have wished for on my last day in the desert. I'm very sensitive to the smell of gas; it makes me feel nauseous. So I practiced walking meditation around the gas station. It helped to keep my spirits up. Ruth was very interested in what was happening at the gas station. She spent a while in the store looking at things and talking to people.

When we left the gas station in Ruth's huge old Chevrolet and continued on with the various errands in town, Ruth would periodically look over at me and ask, "Annabelle, are you aware that you're sitting?" I didn't need to answer, but I focused on feeling the sensation of my body pressing into the seat. I relaxed and let go of the idea that I'd much rather take a walk in the desert. Ruth's presence helped me to become present. The wish to be in a different place or to do something different from what we were doing began to subside.

At the end of the day, Ruth suggested that we go

swimming in the hot springs at Desert Hot Springs, a town on our way back home. I didn't feel like swimming, but I knew that Ruth could relax in the hot water and find relief from her backache. So, I said, "Good idea. You'll go swimming, and I'll sit in one of the deck chairs." It was one of the most wonderful hours of my life. I just sat and listened to the sounds of children playing in the water and the chirping of birds in the palms. I was aware of the sensations in my whole body. I felt a gentle, soft energy inside me. A great feeling of well-being and deep peace filled my body and mind. I was enjoying the fruits of my practice; I'd been mindful and didn't cling to preconceived ideas. I was truly happy during the whole trip home through the mountains to Copper Mesa.

The following guided meditation can help you practice with the Five Spiritual Faculties. May they develop into true strengths to help you transform suffering and nourish joy within yourself and others.

Breathing in, I'm aware that I'm breathing in.
Breathing out, I'm aware that I'm breathing out.

Breathing in, I feel the energy of trust within me.
Breathing out, I smile at the energy of trust.

Breathing in, I feel the strength of my commitment to my spiritual practice.
Breathing out, I enjoy the strength of my commitment.

Breathing in, I feel the energy of mindfulness alive in me.
Breathing out, I smile at the energy of mindfulness within me.

Breathing in, I feel the energy of concentration within me.
Breathing out, I enjoy the energy of concentration within me.

Breathing in, I feel the energy of deep understanding within me.
Breathing out, I smile at the energy of understanding.

Breathing in, I know that the five spiritual faculties can develop into real spiritual strengths that will help myself and others.
Breathing out, I smile at the five spiritual faculties in me.

Breathing in, I am aware of the preciousness of my spiritual practice.
Breathing out, I smile.

18

The Body Mind Connection

OUR BODIES AND MINDS affect each other. They are not separate. Calming the body calms the mind and calming the mind calms the body. The breath is the bridge between body and mind. Conscious breathing brings the wandering mind back to the body and we become truly present here and now.

It's good to pause and become still at various times throughout the day in order to feel your whole body taking a deep in-breath and out-breath. This wonderful practice allows you to become fully aware of the state of your mind. In this stillness, you can mindfully observe your emotional reaction to the mental formation that's taking place and see how it's being expressed in your body.

You may feel how fear makes you freeze, shake, break out in a sweat, or constrict your throat. You might observe how feelings of depression make your body feel heavy or lethargic. You may notice how joyful and happy feelings give you a sense of lightness and ease. You may also experience how feelings of equanimity and serenity make your steps much more stable as you walk.

Understanding the relationship between the mind and the body can help you recognize and put a stop to a habitual reaction. You can notice beneficial mental formations, those that provide peace and happiness, and see how they manifest in your body. You can invite them, like welcome guests, to stay as long as possible. You can also perceive unwholesome mental formations, those that will cause suffering for yourself and others. You can see how they affect your body. You can embrace them with compassion and help their transformation so they won't make you suffer any longer. You can also notice neutral mental formations and feel them in your body.

If you can detect the effects of different mental formations in your body, you have a good set of tools to help you identify which qualities you want to nourish and which you want to transform. This practice can help you to stay open, be curious about life, and find joy in everything you encounter in yourself and around you.

The following guided meditation can help us to understand the body and mind connection:

Breathing in, I'm aware I'm breathing in.
Breathing out, I'm aware I'm breathing out.

Breathing in, I feel the whole length of my in-breath.
Breathing out, I feel the whole length of my
out-breath.

Breathing in, I'm aware of my whole body.
Breathing out, I calm my body.

Breathing in, calming my body helps calm the
functions of my mind.
Breathing out, joy emerges.

Breathing in, I'm aware of the mental formation
of joy.
Breathing out, I feel the joy in my body.

Breathing in, I'm aware of the mental formation
of calmness.
Breathing out, I feel calmness in my body.

*Breathing in, I'm aware of the mental formation
of despair.
Breathing out, I feel how despair is expressed in my
body, and I embrace it with compassion.*

*Breathing in, I'm aware of the mental formation
of fear.
Breathing out, I feel how fear is expressed in my
body, and I embrace it with compassion.*

*Breathing in, I'm aware of the mental formation
of anger.
Breathing out, I feel how anger is expressed in my
body, and I embrace it with compassion.*

*Breathing in, I will recognize and nourish the
wholesome mental formations within me.
Breathing out, I will embrace and transform the
unwholesome mental formations within me.*

*Breathing in, I'm aware that I'm breathing in.
Breathing out, I'm aware that I'm breathing out.*

19

Opening Up to Physical Pain

MOST OF US have never been taught how to deal with physical pain in a positive way. Emotional pain often arises as a result of physical pain, and this can cause us to suffer. We suffer because our mind builds a resistance against the unpleasant feeling of physical pain. The mind says that this pain shouldn't be there. But it's a simple fact that we will all experience physical pain and illness at various times throughout our lives. No one can escape this fact. The body is not set up to exclusively produce pleasant feelings; there will also be unpleasant feelings.

You can take a pain pill in an effort to numb the pain, but in some situations this might not be an option. When you suffer from severe chronic pain, for example, the side effects of the pain medications may hurt your internal organs and cause more damage to your body. And, sometimes the pain is so strong that there aren't any medications that can ease it.

When you're first dealing with pain, you should try to become aware of the painful sensations and be willing to feel them in the moment. It's a good idea to start this practice with minor physical pains first so the practice will be easier when you're faced with major physical pain. (You should always see a doctor when you're experiencing intense physical pain to determine its cause.) You can ask yourself, "Can I truly feel this pain?" "Can I be open to this pain?" "Can I let this pain happen?" When you focus on the pain, you can see if it is concentrated in one area or dispersed throughout the body. Is the pain dull, piercing, burning, or pulsing? When you breathe in, does the pain grow stronger, weaker, or stay the same?

Adopting an open, compassionate attitude toward pain is one of the most important steps you can take toward suffering less. You may ask yourself, "Can I face these unpleasant feelings with compassion?" It can be fascinating to feel what happens in the painful area when you ask this question. Does the painful feeling change when you ask the question? You can also embrace the painful area with great tenderness; you can literally declare your love, even if it might sound false in the beginning. You might say, "My dear, dear stomach, I love you even though you're causing me pain." This declaration of love can also help to dissolve your resistance to the pain.

After you've carefully investigated pain, you can move your attention to a different or more distant area in your body where there are neutral or pleasant sensations. For example, when you're experiencing a headache you can focus instead on the sensations in your feet or hands. This helps enlarge your field of perception; the pain is no longer the only thing in your mind. You allow the pain a wide space in which it can exist with other sensations. Sometimes the pain dissolves when you give it more space, and sometimes it stays the same. At the end of this practice, you should be aware of feeling your entire body one more time and smile at it kindly, so that all the cells in your body may relax as much as possible.

There will be opportunities throughout your life when you can practice with pain in a mindful, open, and compassionate way. This practice can bring peace, equanimity, and stability to your mind. Instead of reacting to physical pain with a "fight or flight" response, you learn how to stay present with pain and see how it may dissolve when you no longer resist it.

The following guided meditation can help you develop an open, compassionate attitude toward pain:

Breathing in, I'm aware I'm breathing in.
Breathing out, I'm aware I'm breathing out.

Breathing in, I'm aware of my whole body.
Breathing out, I calm my body.

Breathing in, I feel a painful area in my body.
Breathing out, I open up to the pain I'm feeling.

Breathing in, I explore my pain.
Breathing out, I discern whether the pain is diffuse,
pulsing, pressing, or pulling.

Breathing in, I ask, "Can I embrace this painful
area with compassion?"
Breathing out, I feel how the question affects
the pain.

Breathing in, I know if the pain increases or
decreases during my in-breath.
Breathing out, I know if the pain increases or
decreases during my out-breath.

*Breathing in, I'm aware of an area in my body that
is free of pain.
Breathing out, I enjoy this feeling of well-being in
my body.*

*Breathing in, I'm aware of my whole body.
Breathing out, I calm my body and smile to it.*

20

Handling Wishes and Desires

Take heed, where are you headed,
heaven is right within you,
Looking for it elsewhere,
you will go astray, again and again.
—Angelus Silesius

The Buddha spoke of five types of wishes and desires that can cause a great amount of suffering if all we do is strive to fulfill them. These desires are to be wealthy, to be powerful, to indulge in sexual excess, to crave large amounts of delicious food, and the desire to do nothing and be slothful. You can witness how the energy of these desires causes tension within. Usually you can feel this tension distinctly in different areas of your body. If you're unaware of your craving or if you hold on to it, the tension may cause you to become blocked and lose your natural openness. You might chase after these desires for your entire life, which will cause a tremendous amount of stress. If you look closely, you'll notice that any fulfilled wish will only bring a brief moment of gratification. Shortly afterward, a new desire arises. Wilhelm Busch said it quite succinctly: "Every desire, in the moment of his fulfillment begets children." This means that every desire, once fulfilled, produces a new desire. Is it possible for us to become aware of the impermanent and empty nature of the objects we desire? If you can cultivate awareness and smile at these desires, they won't control you any longer.

When I speak of craving or desire I'm not talking about basic needs, such as food when you're hungry, warm clothes when it's cold, a place to call home, the ability to visit the doctor when you're sick. I'm referring to unnecessary desires, such as striving to achieve power or riches. Mindfulness helps you to overcome the powerful clinging to unnecessary desires. Through your practice, you'll find greater balance and ease, which will allow you to let go of wishes and desires.

Eating is a good example. You know that eating may bring suffering or happiness depending on your habit energies and how mindful you are of them. When I gulp down food and crave more and more of it, it will lead to extra weight. Obesity greatly raises the risk for many illnesses. If I refuse to eat, on the other hand, I could starve to death. When I eat mindfully, paying attention to chewing, tasting, and swallowing, eating becomes a wonderful process. When the mind focuses simply on eating, then joy and peace will result from this concentration. After I've eaten in this way I feel good in my body and in my mind.

Some people complete one college degree after another believing that they need to gather more training and more certificates. They experience continuous stress and can't be present for their families and friends. Others are workaholics, addicted to their work, unable to sit down and have a cup of tea. They often lose the ability to savor the joys of life.

There are many people who suffer from shopping addiction. They may always be looking for the next best deal and accumulating various collections they don't really need. They might even go into debt due to compulsive shopping, creating a great amount of additional stress that leads to despair and sleepless nights. Whenever I happen to notice myself turning into a greedy consumer, I try to interrupt my attachment to the objects of my desire. It's a good exercise to walk through a shopping mall and buy just one item that you really need. Simply smile at everything else! You'll feel the joy of freedom when you leave the mall and head home with this one item.

The primary objects of my attachment for me are books. As a youth I devoured books. I became oblivious to the world when I read an exciting book. Sometimes my addiction to reading still catches up with me today, especially when I'm reading well-written biographies. When I become aware of this, I put the book aside, feel my breath, and go for a walk or mindfully clean my kitchen to get away from the book for a bit.

The following guided meditation helps us to deal with our desires in a mindful way:

Breathing in, I feel the whole length of my in-breath. Breathing out, I feel the whole length of my out-breath.

Breathing in, I feel the desire for wealth within me. Breathing out, I know that wealth won't bring me true happiness, and I smile at my desire to be wealthy.

Breathing in, I notice my desire to have power over people and things.
Breathing out, I know that power over people and things won't bring me true happiness. I smile at my wish for power.

Breathing in, I feel the desire for sexual gratification.
Breathing out, I'm willing to deal mindfully with my sexual desire, and I smile at it.

Breathing in, I feel the desire for delicious food.
Breathing out, I'm willing to eat mindfully and slowly, so I will satisfy my hunger without eating too much.

Breathing in, I enjoy one piece of chocolate.
Breathing out, I smile at the leftover bar of chocolate.

Breathing in, when I want to do nothing at all, I'll ask if this might be lethargy or depression.
Breathing out, I embrace my feelings.

Breathing in, I feel the drive to be active and work all the time.
Breathing out, I simply sit and watch the clouds drift by.

Breathing in, I feel the urge to watch television.
Breathing out, I smile at the television and don't
turn it on.

Breathing in, I'm aware of my feet as I walk through
the shopping mall.
Breathing out, I get the one item that I came to buy,
and I smile at all the other products.

Breathing in, I enjoy the full length of my in-breath.
Breathing out, I'm willing to bring mindfulness to
my desires.

21

The Four Sources of Nourishment

SHARIPUTRA, a close disciple of the Buddha, gave an important Dharma talk about the four sources of nourishment that we consume. The first source of nourishment is the edible foods and drinks we put in our bodies. We should be mindful and only consume healthy food that doesn't harm the body or mind, other beings, or the environment. The second source of nourishment is the sensory impressions that we're constantly taking in. Sensory impressions penetrate us through our five senses of sight, hearing, smell, taste, and touch. Unless we're sleeping or meditating, these senses are always active and can keep us on our toes. The human mind has the tendency to chase pleasurable sense impressions and avoid unpleasant ones. To escape the sensory overload in our media society, you can choose to live simply and consume radio, television, and newspapers sparingly. You can also choose to spend more time in nature and less time in the city where there may be unwholesome distractions.

The third source of our nourishment is volition, the wholesome or unwholesome intention or motive behind our actions. If you want to experience peace and happiness in your life, it's important to cultivate wholesome intentions within you. This is an important intention to cultivate in a society characterized by superficiality, self-centeredness, violence, revenge, deception, and manipulation. It's infinitely good for you and it has a wonderful effect on all your relationships. If I'm always willing to be open and to be there for others without hurting them through my words and deeds, my life will have a deeper meaning. The cultivation of wholesome intentions requires your clarity of mind, generosity, patience, and deep understanding. We all have challenging habit energies, but it's possible to become aware of them and transform them, so we can be in touch with our deeper, more wholesome motivations.

The fourth source of nourishment is individual and collective consciousness. It's very helpful to practice with others. It encourages you to cultivate your own wholesome seeds. Some of your co-practitioners may inspire you with their exceptional goodness, compassion, equanimity, serenity, and generosity. Others may challenge you, because they're impatient, judgmental, or angry. You have to be very aware of how much negativity you're willing to absorb, especially when you're just beginning on this path and your wholesome seeds may not be strong. When you're just beginning to develop mindfulness and cultivate your positive qualities such as kindness, compassion, equanimity, understanding, and mindfulness, it's important to spend time with people who can inspire you. The Buddha called such people "our noble friends." Spending time at a Buddhist monastery or retreat center can be a good place to begin to receive inspiration and guidance from other laypeople, monks, and nuns. In this setting you have the opportunity to watch people practicing mindfulness while they are cleaning, gardening and cooking, when they communicate with each other, and when they're faced with difficult situations.

One year during the summer retreat in Plum Village, the sound system for the translations wasn't working. People from many countries come to Plum Village in the summer to hear Thich Nhat Hanh's talks translated into their native language. I watched the monks who were responsible for the sound system that day walking slowly from one translation station to another, checking the cables. Nhat Hanh sat in the front of the hall and signed a pile of books. Even after he'd signed them all, the system still wasn't working. He didn't say anything. He simply sat in silence and the several hundred people in the hall sat with him. It was wonderful. This lasted for approximately fifty minutes. In those moments, the quiet energy of the monks and nuns was transferred to us on a cellular level. They passed on the wonderful practice of mindfulness, concentration, equanimity, compassion, and understanding. Being in the midst of a community of practitioners, a Sangha, can benefit your practice greatly.

The following guided meditation supports the awareness and practice of the four sources of our nourishment. With greater awareness we will lead a purposeful life in mindfulness and with compassion for our society and ourselves.

Breathing in, I'm aware that I'm breathing in.
Breathing out, I'm aware that I'm breathing out.

*Breathing in, I'm willing only to accept nourishment
that won't harm myself and others.
Breathing out, I smile.*

*Breathing in, I'm willing to develop stability and
create a calm environment for myself.
Breathing out, I enjoy the simple things in life.*

*Breathing in, I listen to the chirping of cicadas on
a balmy summer night.
Breathing out, I smile.*

*Breathing in, I watch the snowflakes fall on a quiet
winter morning.
Breathing out, I smile.*

*Breathing in, I want to share the simple joys in life
with others.
Breathing out, I invite a friend for a walk in nature.*

*Breathing in, I know that the energy of people who
live in mindfulness and equanimity helps me to lead
a more mindful and joyful life.
Breathing out, I smile.*

*Breathing in, I want to develop clarity
and understanding.*

Breathing out, I won't allow others to draw me into negative ways of thinking, speaking, and acting.

Breathing in, I want to develop equanimity and compassion.
Breathing out, I offer comfort.

Breathing in, I want to stay calm even in difficult situations.
Breathing out, I offer friendliness to someone who's upset.

Breathing in, I want to develop wholesome intentions for the well-being of myself and all beings.
Breathing out, I smile and feel how beneficial this will be for me and for others.

22

Recognizing Our Ancestors

THE BUDDHA teaches that there is no independent, separate self; everything that exists is dependent on everything else that exists. We only exist because of our parents and they exist because of our grandparents and an endless line of ancestors.

In Western culture, we're very concerned about independence and individuality and are often proud of it. This preoccupation might lead us to cut ourselves off from others because they're different from us in some way. But this strategy of separation, which we supposed would bring us greater happiness, may actually lead to suffering and feelings of isolation and loneliness. If we don't have close relationships, or we only have a few relationships, we can suffer. If we don't reach out to others or let them touch us, we might be overcome by feelings of sorrow and despair.

It's helpful to seek connection with your blood relatives (parents, grandparents) and your spiritual ancestors (all those who have supported you on the path of understanding and love). It helps to stay connected to the ancestors of your country (those who created the infrastructure, the laws, and the culture) and to renew and deepen this bond. When you do this, you see that you are much more than a tiny isolated drop of water, and rather are part of a great stream of beings that has been flowing since time immemorial and will keep flowing for a very long time. If you understand and feel deeply that you're part of humanity and the whole universe, you may regain a sense of security that you might have lost over the course of your life.

You consist of many elements and energies that came to you from your parents and ancestors. You have been given many wonderful energies, but you've also been given some difficult energies. Practicing mindfulness helps you to recognize which of your ancestors' energies are wholesome. Maybe your mother or father were compassionate, caring, modest, and generous. You should appreciate those wholesome energies and nurture them within yourself. Mindfulness will also help you to see which thoughts, words, and actions of your ancestors bring suffering. Maybe your mother or father criticized you frequently and used disparaging words. Maybe they humiliated you through physical punishment or even sexual abuse. Those are the types of energies you want to transform so they won't continue any longer. You can practice embracing yourself through compassion to gradually ease the pain of these wounds.

Your spiritual ancestors also transmitted their positive and negative energies to you. I always like to remember the pastor in my hometown, who was such a good and compassionate person. I also remember my mother, who came to our bed every night to pray with us when we were young children. These prayers helped me to surrender all my worries to a higher power.

When you think about your cultural ancestors, you envision all the people who worked hard to build the infrastructure of your homeland, but you also remember the cruelty, vindictiveness, and violence that have existed in your history. The more you become aware of the difficult energies handed down by your cultural ancestors and the more ready you are to transform them, the less you need to fear that they will dominate you and that you will pass them on either consciously or unconsciously.

You can also view all the food you eat as your ancestors; everything you eat and drink keeps you alive. The earth, water, air, sun, and moon all contribute to the origin and growth of the food we eat. All these energies play their part in keeping you alive—you wouldn't exist without them.

The following guided meditation can help you become aware of the energies of your ancestors and transform the feelings of loneliness and isolation that many of us experience.

Breathing in, I'm aware that I'm breathing in.
Breathing out, I'm aware that I'm breathing out.

Breathing in, I'm aware of my mother's wonderful energies.
Breathing out, I smile at my mother's wonderful energies within me.

Breathing in, I'm aware of my mother's difficult energies.

*Breathing out, I smile with compassion at my
mother's difficult energies within me.*

*Breathing in, I'm aware of my father's wonderful
energies.*
*Breathing out, I smile at my father's wonderful
energies within me.*

*Breathing in, I'm aware of my father's difficult
energies.*
*Breathing out, I smile with compassion at my
father's difficult energies within me.*

*Breathing in, I'm aware of the wonderful energies
of my spiritual ancestors.*
*Breathing out, I offer compassion to the weaknesses
of my spiritual ancestors.*

*Breathing in, I'm aware of all the wonderful energies
of my cultural ancestors.*
*Breathing out, I'm ready to transform the difficult
energies of my cultural ancestors within me.*

*Breathing in, I'm aware of the countless elements
that nourish me in the form of food today.*
*Breathing out, I give thanks to all these energies and
smile at them.*

Breathing in, I remember all the energies (earth, water, air, sun, farmers) that helped to grow the food that nourished me today.
Breathing out, I give thanks to all these energies and smile to them.

Breathing in, I feel the solidity of the earth beneath me.
Breathing out, I feel connected to all the beings who live and share the earth with me in this moment, and I smile to them.

23

Awareness of Feelings

LOOKING DEEPLY at feelings (*vedana*) is part of the second foundation of mindfulness, understanding the causes of suffering. In this context, a feeling isn't the same as an emotion. A feeling is your awareness at any given moment that what you're experiencing is either a pleasant, unpleasant, or neutral sensation.

When you are first examining a feeling, bring your awareness to the physical body. What can I perceive and identify with my five senses? Is what I'm feeling, smelling, seeing, tasting, or hearing pleasant, unpleasant, or neutral? Notice that the mind has a tendency to always seek out pleasant sensations and try to escape unpleasant ones. It's always on the run. For this reason, we recognize neutral sensations less often, despite the fact that most sensations we experience during the course of a day tend to be neutral.

Mental formations like kindness, compassion, joy,

equanimity, and generosity are pleasant. Unrest, agitation, despair, anger, pride, or feelings of inferiority are unpleasant and lead to suffering when they dominate your mind or when you act on them or suppress them. Neutral feelings refer to a state when you feel neither joy nor anger. Usually you're not aware of neutral feelings. But with awareness, they can become positive feelings. Washing the dishes, sitting on the bus, or brushing your teeth can be enjoyable experiences. Calling to mind the impermanence of pleasant, unpleasant, and neutral feelings helps you refrain from clinging to what's pleasant or running away from unpleasant feelings.

It's a good exercise to focus on the various "shades of feelings" you experience for a day or even a week and to determine whether they are pleasant, unpleasant, or neutral. It might look like any of the following scenarios:

▸ A dharma friend calls me and wants to talk about a difficult situation. I listen, ask her questions, and give my opinion. It helps her to understand the situation better. She has more clarity about her situation and is relieved. She says, "Talking to you really helped me. Thank you so much." Her words of appreciation bring a pleasant feeling to my mind.

▸ One of my housemates says in a slightly irritated voice, "That really annoyed me when you…" I notice a feeling of irritation arising within me, which I identify as an unpleasant feeling.

▸ I cut myself a piece of bread and I notice how simple this action is. It leaves me with a neutral feeling. But when I become aware of the miracle of the bread, of cutting it, and of having enough to eat, my neutral feeling becomes a pleasant feeling.

The practice of mindfulness helps you observe your pleasant, unpleasant, or neutral feelings without reacting to them in the way you would habitually do. This practice creates more space in your mind so you're able to react in a peaceful, compassionate, kind, and calm way in any given situation.

One beautiful summer day I went for a walk at Lake Lietzen in a park near the apartment where I lived at the time. The lake sparkled in the sun, children played in the grass, people sat on benches and on the grass, and a light summer breeze blew through the bushes and trees. The atmosphere was very peaceful.

I was in an excellent mood and all I wanted to do was to sit down on a bench, feel my breath, and enjoy the beautiful day. All the benches were taken, however. A middle-aged man was sitting alone on one of them. When I came closer to the man, I realized why no one was sharing the bench with him. He smelled strongly of alcohol and urine. I noticed an unpleasant feeling arising. I named the feeling in my mind "unpleasant feeling." I knew from my mindfulness training that thoughts of running away follow right on the heel of unpleasant feelings. Then, I remembered a few sentences from the metta meditation about offering unconditional love to all beings "large or small, long or short"—or "smelling pleasant or unpleasant," I added in my mind. I felt encouraged to practice right there in that moment with this man.

I said hello and asked if I could sit next to him. He seemed very happy that I'd asked to sit there and we started to talk. I felt my breath and listened to his life story. He had worked in a slaughterhouse and eventually could no longer stand inflicting that kind of pain on innocent animals. He heard them scream in his sleep and felt their fear and despair. He began to drink and gave up his job at the slaughterhouse. He never really found another job. He was only able to find temporary work because he had become addicted to alcohol. Drinking seemed to be the only way to escape his pain.

I was very touched by his story and thanked him for his openness. He was really happy that I'd listened. He didn't feel excluded from the peaceful park atmosphere any longer.

The following meditation can help you become aware of our pleasant, unpleasant, and neutral feelings:

Breathing in, I'm aware that I'm breathing in.
Breathing out, I'm aware that I'm breathing out.

Breathing in, I'm aware of pleasant feelings in my body.
Breathing out, I'm aware of the impermanence of these pleasant feelings and I smile to them.

Breathing in, I'm aware of unpleasant feelings in my body.
Breathing out, I'm aware of the impermanence of these unpleasant feelings and I smile to them.

*Breathing in, I'm aware of neutral feelings in
my body.
Breathing out, I'm aware of the impermanence
of these neutral feelings and smile.*

*Breathing in, I'm aware of pleasant
mental formations.
Breathing out, I nurture them and smile.*

*Breathing in, I'm aware of unpleasant
mental formations.
Breathing out, I face them with patience and smile.*

*Breathing in, I'm aware of neutral
mental formations.
Breathing out, I smile and they transform into joy.*

*Breathing in, I listen to the singing of the birds on a
spring morning.
Breathing out, I know that their singing makes me
happy, and I smile to them.*

*Breathing in, I listen to the sound of a tense voice.
Breathing out, I am grateful for my hearing.*

*Breathing in, I'm aware that I'm cutting the bread.
Breathing out, I recognize that I am grateful for
the bread.*

Breathing in, I observe the stream of different feelings inside me.
Breathing out, I smile.

24
Neutral Feelings and the Possibility of Joy

THE FOLLOWING guided meditation can help you become aware of neutral feelings in your body and mind. You can practice embracing these feelings with joy. You become aware of the things you usually take for granted and of your connection to others who do not have these things.

Thich Nhat Hanh points out that awareness of neutral feelings gives us an occasion to feel joyful. If we remember the hard times in our life then when we experience neutral feelings we have the opportunity to feel gratitude. It's a chance for us to delight as these neutral feelings become positive feelings simply by bringing our awareness to them.

Sometimes we don't have the courage to enjoy our neutral feelings because we know that others in the world are suffering. Millions of people are afflicted by depression, despair, greed, jealousy, vindictiveness, and hatred, while your own mind may be at ease, calm, and peaceful. Many people sit in a wheelchair, while you may be able to walk. You may have plenty to eat, while millions of people suffer from hunger and thirst. You may be healthy and have clean water to drink, while many people get sick or die because of malnutrition and lack of clean drinking water.

When you're in a neutral state, and you become aware of this neutral state, you can open your heart to all the people who suffer from physical or mental pain and find themselves in depressing, difficult situations. You can explore what you might do to ease the suffering of those who live close by or even those who are far away.

Breathing in, I'm aware that I'm breathing in.
Breathing out, I'm aware that I'm breathing out.

*Breathing in, I'm aware that I don't have a
headache right now.*
Breathing out, this awareness makes me happy.

*Breathing in, I'm aware that I don't have any pain
in my knees.*

Breathing out, this awareness makes me happy.

Breathing in, I'm aware that I am not living in a situation of war right now and I am grateful for this. Breathing out, I send compassion to all beings who suffer in situations of war right now.

Breathing in, I know that I will have enough to eat today and I am happy that I won't go hungry. Breathing out, I send compassion to all beings who are hungry today.

*Breathing in, I feel the gentle summer breeze on my face.
Breathing out, I smile.*

*Breathing in, I hear the sounds of children playing in the distance.
Breathing out, I smile.*

*Breathing in, I'm aware of the preciousness of my practice of mindfulness and compassion.
Breathing out, I enjoy this moment.*

25
Difficult Feelings

It's important to pay attention to difficult feelings as they arise and not ignore or suppress them. To deal with these difficult feelings, you first of all want to become aware of the mental formations that are arising in the present moment. It doesn't help to chase them away by saying, "I'm not really angry," or "I'm not disappointed, greedy, or in despair." It's more productive to admit that these feelings are present within us.

Secondly, during these moments it's helpful to practice walking meditation and feel your breath and the physical sensations as you breathe in and out. This gives you a chance to be in touch with things that are neutral or pleasant. Both body and mind will feel renewed and more stable after only a few minutes.

Thirdly, embrace your difficult mental formations with compassion, patience, and understanding. Gradually, you see that cultivating mindfulness, compassion, and understanding grants freedom from being overwhelmed by negative feelings. You're able to stop repeating the story that gave rise to these feelings. Finally you can change the tape in your head that's been playing the same melody over and over again.

If you keep practicing with your difficult emotions as soon as they arise, their seeds will be weakened as they return to store consciousness. You start to heal on a much deeper level. Old patterns that led to continuous suffering begin to dissolve.

We all have seeds of negative thoughts and feelings in our store consciousness. Under certain conditions these negative seeds might develop into deep despondence or even clinical depression. Our negative seeds get watered every time something doesn't work the way we expect or someone acts in a way that we perceive as undesirable or even hurtful. The unwholesome seeds also receive nourishment when we aren't content with our partner, at work, or with life in general. It's important that we recognize negative thoughts as they arise. It's good to label them as such, to name them as exactly what they are: jealousy, anger, and so on.

You can observe the way your negative thoughts translate into physical sensations. Be aware of them as you follow your in-breath and out-breath. But you don't have to let these thoughts propel you along a downward emotional spiral. While this might have happened countless times in the past, you are better prepared now. You can ask, "Can I offer compassion to myself when I have these negative thoughts that make me suffer?" Asking the question can interrupt your habitual way of reacting to a difficult situation with negative thoughts. The question also expresses your understanding that your store consciousness, where all mental formations originate, holds positive mental formations as well. These positive mental formations, such as mindfulness, patience, and compassion, can come to embrace and aid the more difficult mental formations.

Give yourself permission to refrain from reacting to the negative situation. You can say to yourself, "I'm willing or I vow to stop these negative thoughts now." Then turn towards something neutral; you might feel the sensation of your feet touching the ground as you walk along the street or climb the stairs. You might focus on how you open the door or brush your teeth.

This helps to interrupt the negative thoughts and it stabilizes your mind.

If it was another person who contributed to your irritation and negative thoughts, you can try to put yourself in that person's shoes. It's best to wait until your mind has become quiet, calm, and stable before you talk to the other person. You should try to find friendly words for what you want to communicate. Words that hurt or blame aren't helpful at all. You want to keep the channel of communication open.

The following guided meditation can help you recognize and heal negative difficult feelings:

Breathing in, I'm aware that I'm breathing in.
Breathing out, I'm aware that I'm breathing out.

Breathing in, I feel the full length of my in-breath.
Breathing out, I enjoy the full length of my
out-breath.

Every conscious in-breath brings freshness to my
body and mind.
Every conscious out-breath helps me to let go.

Breathing in, I'm aware of feeling disappointed.

Breathing out, I embrace my disappointment with compassion.

Breathing in, I'm aware of feeling angry.
Breathing out, I embrace my anger with compassion.

Breathing in, I'm aware of feeling despair.
Breathing out, I embrace my despair with compassion.

Breathing in, I'm aware of feeling insecure.
Breathing out, I embrace my insecurity with compassion.

Breathing in, I'm aware of a feeling of greed.
Breathing out, I embrace my greed with compassion.

Breathing in, I'm aware that mindfulness and compassion are in me.
Breathing out, I smile at my mindfulness and compassion.

Breathing in, I'm aware that my practice of mindfulness and compassion is precious.
Breathing out, I smile.

26

Dealing with Life's Ups and Downs

ONE DAY when I was cleaning up my desk at work, I started to become overwhelmed with all the piles of papers, notes, lectures, business correspondence, bank statements, and bills covering my desk. I began to notice myself slowly spiraling into a minor panic attack. I said to myself, "Annabelle, just relax, breathe, and smile. In forty years, worms will crawl all over your bones and play hide and seek in your eye sockets." This could have upset me more, but instead it helped me to put my own panic in perspective. It made the things that I was worrying about seem less crucial than life or death.

The piles on my desk pale in comparison to the truly difficult situations some people find themselves in. My practice puts my situation in perspective. It transforms my despair so that I no longer identify with it. I collect myself and begin to look at the papers on my desk. Checking one document after another mindfully, I sort them in various piles. I'll attend to some papers right away, and the others I won't get to for a while. Most of the time I'll toss out any papers that have been sitting around for more than two months.

The Mahamangala Sutta (The Discourse on Happiness) reads: "To live in the world with your heart undisturbed by the world, with all sorrows ended, dwelling in peace—this is the greatest happiness." But time and again we are affected by what the Buddha called the "eight worldly winds." These winds are four pairs of opposites: pleasure and pain, success and failure, gain and loss, and praise and blame. They touch us gently and cradle us, or they push, shake, and greatly upset us. It's important that we learn to deal with them skillfully. We are always attracted to the favorable winds of pleasure, success, gain, and praise, and we do everything we can to stay in these states. This is only natural. But they may carry us away so that we begin to feel pride, arrogance, self-righteousness, and superiority to others. These attitudes will only feed the unwholesome and painful feelings within us. While we're experiencing the joy of the favorable winds, we need to pay attention to the feelings they create in us.

The less favorable winds of pain, failure, loss, and blame almost always cause suffering. We experience these winds as unpleasant and they make us feel insecure. They can lead us to despair, anger, a desire for revenge, feelings of inferiority, and depression. If we experience a misfortune, failure, loss, or criticism, it often feels like so much is beyond our control. Not many can honestly say in these moments, "Oh well, this is just one of the worldly winds almost blowing me over."

The only way to practice with these unpleasant winds is to not suppress the difficult feelings that they cause to whirl up within you. It's good to observe them and hold them in mindfulness. You can ask yourself, "Can I feel these emotions in my body? Am I hot with anger? Does my throat feel constricted with fear? Do I feel weak from despair?" Then return to your breath. Breathing in and breathing out in awareness, you dissolve some of the resistance against the unpleasant feelings.

These unpleasant worldly winds provide a wonderful opportunity to develop compassion for yourself and others. If you can offer unconditional compassion to your fear, despair, anger, or feeling of inferiority, you can stop the identification with these feelings and keep them from escalating. The usual drama is then interrupted. In the very moment you can embrace despair with mindfulness and compassion, it no longer runs amok in your body and mind. Despair is now in the hands of two good friends, mindfulness and compassion, and they will help it to dissolve. You can relax in the midst of a difficult, worldly wind. There's no need to be afraid of it any longer.

The following guided meditation can help you deal with the ups and downs in life more skillfully. Practicing in this way you become less entangled in the painful reactions that cause suffering in yourself and others.

Breathing in, I know I'm breathing in.
Breathing out, I know I'm breathing out.

Every intentional in-breath gives me stability.
Every intentional out-breath gives me equanimity.

Breathing in, I'm aware of a misfortune or failure.
Breathing out, I embrace myself with compassion.

Breathing in, I am aware of feeling criticized.
Breathing out, I embrace myself and all those who felt attacked or criticized today.

Breathing in, I'm aware of all the people who have experienced a misfortune today.
Breathing out, I feel connected with all these people and I smile to them.

Breathing in, I'm aware of a loss in my life.
Breathing out, I smile to myself with compassion.

Breathing in, I'm aware of all the people who have suffered a loss today.
Breathing out, I feel connected with all people.

27

Are Our Perceptions Accurate?

THE BUDDHA SAID we should continuously check our perceptions, because many of them are wrong or inadequate. He describes six types of perceptions:

1. The perception pertaining to the sight of colors and forms
2. The perception pertaining to the hearing of sounds
3. The perception pertaining to the smelling of odors
4. The perception pertaining to taste
5. The perception pertaining to the feeling of touch
6. The perception pertaining to thinking or objects of mind

The Buddha points out that wherever there are perceptions, there will be deceptions, which will eventually lead to suffering. When you ask fifteen people the same question about the same situation, you'll probably end up with fifteen different stories. You need to be careful when perceptions come into play. So many arguments in relationships are caused by different perceptions. Instead of insisting on being right—an attitude that leads to suffering on both sides—you can simply smile at each other and say, "Oh, we obviously have very different perceptions."

At the end of a seminar I attended, I listened to several comments about one of the participants. People had many different perceptions. One person said, "He made several good points during our discussion. I found his participation enriching." Another person said, "I didn't like him at all. He must be from a Nazi family." A third person said, "He seemed so familiar to me with his dark curly hair. He reminded me of a little boy whose half-Jewish mother hid at my Aunt Ilse's house during the Holocaust." A fourth person said, "We started talking during one of the breaks. First, I found it very difficult to talk to him, but later he told me a few stories from his childhood and I began to understand him better. I was very touched and my aversion dissolved completely."

Thich Nhat Hanh advises that you should always ask two questions about your perceptions: "Can I be sure that my perception is correct?" and "Can I really be sure?" It's important to realize that your perceptions are influenced by your habit energies, which have been passed down from your ancestors, your social environment, your culture, and the collective consciousness of the time in which you live. Only mindfulness of your perceptions and an ongoing exchange with others will help you see how many different perceptions may actually exist in one situation. If you're careless with your perceptions you may cause suffering for yourself and others.

The following guided meditation can help you be mindful of your perceptions and less attached to your expectations.

> *Breathing in, I'm aware of my whole body.*
> *Breathing out, I feel all the sensations and I calm my body.*
>
> *Breathing in, I'm aware of my perceptions in this moment.*
> *Breathing out, I ask, can I be sure of my perceptions?*
>
> *Breathing in, I hear how others perceive the situation.*

*Breathing out, I'm surprised by all the
different perceptions.*

*Breathing in, I'm willing to not insist on
my perceptions.*
*Breathing out, I'm open to looking carefully and
considering the perceptions of others.*

*Breathing in, I'm aware that my perceptions
are influenced by my blood ancestors, spiritual
ancestors, and cultural ancestors.*
Breathing out, I smile to all my ancestors.

*Breathing in, I am aware that people can have
different perceptions.*
*Breathing out, I know there is room for all these
different perceptions.*

28

The Practice of Non-harming

We HAVE ALL been wounded in some way or another by the words and actions of other people during our lifetime. If we're willing to look carefully, we realize that we also have hurt other people either consciously or unconsciously. We often suffer our entire life because of these wounds. And others may be suffering from the injuries that we've inflicted upon them. They might turn away from us and ask not to see us anymore. Hurtful words and behavior can cause us a great deal of unrest, agitation, feelings of inferiority, and guilt.

If you want to invite more peace and happiness into your life, the practice of non-harming is fundamental on your spiritual path. The Buddha's five ethical principles remind us how to act mindfully towards other living beings. They state our commitment to abstain from harming living beings, stealing, sexual misconduct, lying, and intoxication. The principle of abstaining from harming living beings or non-harming is a valuable guideline for all your actions. Others will feel safe and secure in your presence when they know that you won't harm or attack them with your words or behavior.

While the five ethical principles often mirror our imperfections all too well, we can still look to them as guiding stars that lead the way. You should be happy when you achieve major or minor successes in your practice of non-harming. When you notice that you talk much less frequently about others in a negative way, or that you don't use words to belittle anyone, you can feel happy without slipping into pride, being condescending, or being judgmental toward others.

When a friend comes to me and says, "Annabelle, when you said this, I felt really hurt," I'm always sorry. I don't want to hurt anyone, so it's easy for me to say I'm sorry to my friend whether or not I believe that the incident was due to my own shortcomings or to my friend being overly sensitive.

The following guided meditation can help you practice non-harming and nurture happiness and peace within yourself, others, and our society.

Breathing in, I know I'm breathing in.
Breathing out, I know I'm breathing out.

Breathing in, I'm aware of the suffering caused by
killing or physically harming another being.
Breathing out, I vow to practice nonviolence toward
all beings.

Breathing in, I'm aware of the suffering caused by
stealing, exploitation, and injustice in our society.
Breathing out, I vow to never take anything that
belongs to others.

Breathing in, I'm aware of the suffering caused by
unmindful sexual behavior.
Breathing out, I'm determined not to harm others by
my sexual behavior.

Breathing in, I'm aware of the suffering caused by
unmindful, cruel, or judgmental speech
Breathing out, I vow to practice loving speech and to
listen to others with an open heart.

Breathing in, I'm aware of the suffering caused
by drugs, alcohol, certain periodicals, television
programs, and books.

*Breathing out, I am determined to avoid consuming
anything that would obscure my mind.*

*Breathing in, I'm aware that the practice of non-
harming will bring peace, comfort, and happiness to
myself and others.*
*Breathing out, I'm aware of the preciousness of my
practice of non-harming.*

29
Dealing with Sexual Feelings

SEXUAL ENERGY is very powerful. We can learn to work with this strong energy in a relaxed and kind way. The culture around us places a high value on fulfilling our sexual desires. This can create confusion and suffering, both for ourselves and our loved ones. When we are physically intimate with someone without emotionally intimacy, there is a disconnect, an emptiness that opens up within us.

A great deal of advertising in the public media uses sexuality to encourage consumption of everything from clothes and makeup to cars and batteries. Noticing when our sexual energy arises and acknowledging this sexual energy without judgment lessens our sense of urgency and the energy's power. If we look closely we will notice which images, texts, music, or films trigger our sexual energies, and we can acknowledge them.

If we are in an intimate relationship with another person, sexuality may be an important component of that relationship, but it is not the only component. If we focus only on that energy, and don't build emotional intimacy, then we tend to hurt each other and start engaging in sexual activity outside of the relationship. Our suffering will not be eased by engaging in sexuality without intimacy.

When we sense sexual feelings, we can acknowledge them mindfully. We can feel them through our in-breath and our out-breath, and we can relax. There is great freedom in this awareness, in the simple acceptance of feeling what is there.

When people try and run away from their suffering and channel their anger or loneliness through sexuality, pain and suffering arise. This may be what they have experienced around them or seen in others. Vulnerable people, including children, are often victims of sexual abuse and violence. Each of us is responsible not only for being mindful of our own sexuality, but also for taking care that those around us do not suffer from violence or abuse.

The following guided meditation can help us deal

in a kind and relaxed way with our sexual energy as it arises.

Breathing in, I feel sexual energy in my whole body.
Breathing out, I breathe and enjoy the sexual energy in my whole body.

Breathing in, I commit to paying mindful attention to my sexual feelings
Breathing out, I smile.

Breathing in, I am aware how certain images, texts, sounds, and odors arouse sexual feelings in me.
Breathing out, I smile and relax.

Breathing in, I feel how a another person arouses sexual feelings in me.
Breathing out, I smile and relax.

Breathing in, I commit to releasing sexual energy in healthy ways that increase my mindful connection to others.
Breathing out, I know there is no need to rush.

Breathing in, I know that truthfulness is important for my inner peace and balance.
Breathing out, I smile.

Breathing in, I am aware of true beauty around me.
Breathing out, I relax my body and my mind.

Breathing in, I know that a loving partnership can
be a great treasure.
Breathing out, I smile.

30

Developing Appreciation

M OST OF US are familiar with feelings of inferiority. Either you don't really appreciate yourself or you feel that others don't give you enough rec-
ognition. At other times you don't appreciate others
enough. The feeling of "not being good enough" can
come up in many areas in your life. Sometimes you
believe you should be further along on your spiritual
path, in your career, or in your relationships.

When we were children and young adults, some
of us were repeatedly hurt by overly critical, pejora-
tive words spoken either by our family of origin, at
school, during vocational training, or at college. If this
happened to you, you may pass on the same type of
energy to others.

The following guided meditation serves as a reminder of all the good qualities in yourself and in

others. It supports your commitment to appreciate
yourself and others with kindness and understanding.

Breathing in, I know I'm breathing in.
Breathing out, I know I'm breathing out.

Breathing in, I see all the wonderful seeds of
understanding, love, and compassion within me.
Breathing out, I want to develop these seeds and I
smile to myself.

Breathing in, I see the wonderful qualities of
a good friend.
Breathing out, I smile to my friend.

Breathing in, I see the good qualities of
a neutral person.
Breathing out, I smile to this person
with appreciation.

Breathing in, I acknowledge the good qualities
of someone I have a difficult relationship with.
Breathing out, I smile to this person.

Breathing in, I acknowledge the good qualities
of someone I love.
Breathing out, I smile to my loved one.

Breathing in, I acknowledge the good qualities of everyone in this room.
Breathing out, I smile to everyone in the room.

Breathing in, I know that every being carries Buddha nature within.
Breathing out, I smile to all beings.

Breathing in, I'm aware of the preciousness of my spiritual practice.
Breathing out, I smile.

31

Communicating Appreciation

MANY PEOPLE have experienced painful and hurtful relationships in their childhood, youth, and adult life. Most people don't grow up in an environment where nurturing communication and positive interaction exist. Often, due to this personal history, many people have difficulty communicating with others because they're accustomed to focusing on the negative qualities in themselves and in others, creating an experience of separateness, rather than connection.

Thich Nhat Hanh and the Plum Village Sangha developed the practice of Beginning Anew to help practitioners communicate with each other with mindfulness and kindness. The practice provides practitioners with the methods and tools to build stable relationships and skillfully navigate the many storms that arise in relationships. The practice supports you in moving toward the experience of connectedness and away from separateness. Beginning Anew helps you become aware of your own positive qualities that exist in your store consciousness, and to know that other people carry these positive qualities as well.

You can practice Beginning Anew with one person or a group, with a family member, a partner, friend, coworker, members of your spiritual practice group, or anyone else in your circles whenever difficult circumstances arise. Beginning Anew works best when you practice regularly, especially when you're first beginning this practice. You might decide, for example, to meet at least twice a month with your partner, a close friend, or a coworker to take part in this practice. But, of course, this practice only works if both people involved are willing to commit to this type of communication.

In the first part of Beginning Anew, one person talks about the positive characteristics of the other without exaggeration and flattery. This is called "watering the flowers in the other person." You share all the positive things you became aware of during the last week or month. For example, you might say to your partner, "I was so happy that you cleaned the kitchen and washed all the dishes last week when I came home absolutely exhausted." The result of focusing on the positive qualities of another person and expressing them are often astonishing. Regular practice begins to change your perception of the other person completely. Instead of criticizing him or her as you might have done before, you become researchers whose job it is to detect as many positive qualities as possible. You don't want to sit at your next meeting with them and not be able to mention any positive qualities.

When you first practice Beginning Anew, you focus solely on the positive qualities in the other person. This can be practiced for many months, especially in a difficult relationship. It will result in a strong foundation of mutual appreciation. I practiced this way for several months with a friend and it was a great blessing for both of us. We come from very different worlds, but we lived and worked together. It was important for us to get along. If we had decided to have more customary heart-to-hearts in which we listed all the things that weren't going well between us, our relationship might have ended. However, the opposite happened for us. We started to look forward to our "flower-watering" nights when we could express the

many beautiful qualities and features that we'd dis-
covered in each other. This first part of the Beginning
Anew exercise can bring deep healing to a broken
relationship.

In the second part of Beginning Anew, you confess
your mistakes and regrets to the other person. You
apologize for things you said, did, or neglected to do
that may have hurt the other person. For example,
you may say, "I'm sorry that I hurt you with my
judgmental remark. I realized later that this comment
was difficult for you and I shouldn't have spoken in
that way."

In the third part of Beginning Anew, you have an
opportunity to let the other person become aware of
a situation that may be preoccupying you and making
you less available. This can relieve the other person
of any feelings of confusion or guilt that might have
developed or any concern that he or she might some-
how be responsible for your changed behavior. You
may be dealing with other circumstances that have
influenced the way you communicated with the other
person. For example, you may have learned that you
have a serious illness, that you might lose your job,
or that someone close to you needs care or might

not live much longer. These kinds of situations can easily make you anxious, and it's important to share these feelings with the person you're engaging in this practice with. There's no need for the other person to feel guilty or suspect that he or she is responsible for your behavior. You might say, "If I've been sad or less cheerful recently, please don't think that this has anything to do with you or something you have done. It's just very difficult for me to deal with this situation."

In the fourth part of Beginning Anew, you talk about the times when you've felt hurt. Expressing to another person that you've been hurt should happen in a calm way, never in an exaggerated, reproachful, accusatory, or desperate manner. This is about the healing of the relationship, not about hopelessness or breaking up. Before you share how you've been hurt, make sure you feel calm inside. You might even want to practice sitting or walking meditation beforehand. One person expresses his or her feelings of hurt while the other person listens without responding, even if the person who's speaking says something that has resulted from a wrong perception. Then you agree to meet again at another time, so that the other person may speak and present his or her perspective. Some people may want to invite a neutral third person to witness this fourth part of Beginning Anew. Often, the presence of a neutral person in these circumstances can support a mindful and kind interaction.

The following guided meditation can help you to develop appreciation, forgiveness, compassion, and truthfulness in your relationships.[4]

Breathing in, I know I'm breathing in.
Breathing out, I know I'm breathing out.

Breathing in, I see all my positive qualities.
Breathing out, I want to recognize the positive
qualities in my partner, friend, coworker,
or family member.

Breathing in, I want to find many examples of the
positive qualities in my partner, friend, coworker,
or family member and express my appreciation
of him or her.
Breathing out, I feel the joy that my words of
appreciation bring to my partner, friend, coworker,
or family member.

4. The Plum Village Sangha has developed a Peace Treaty supporting mindful and healing ways of handling difficult relationships. See Thich Nhat Hanh, *Fidelity* (Parallax Press, Berkeley, CA: 2011).

Breathing in, I'm willing to recognize how my words or actions may have hurt another person.
Breathing out, I'm willing to apologize to him or her.

Breathing in, I share a difficult situation I'm encountering.
Breathing out, I assure the other person my unusual behavior isn't related to anything that he or she has done.

Breathing in, I'm aware that I feel hurt by someone's words or actions.
Breathing out, I'm willing to calm my mind in sitting or walking meditation.

Breathing in, I ask to talk to my partner, friend, coworker, or family member about my hurt feelings.
Breathing out, I will share my hurt feelings in a calm and friendly manner. I won't accuse or blame the other person.

Breathing in, I feel the joy that comes from communication based on goodwill, truthfulness, and appreciation.
Breathing out, I smile.

32
Buddha Nature

WHEN WE AREN'T doing so well, and we find ourselves embroiled in problems, we can always remember our Buddha nature and access the positive qualities that lie in our store consciousness. These are our own Buddha qualities that live within us. When we acknowledge these seeds of mindfulness, stability, calmness, and openness, we allow these positive seeds to manifest in our conscious mind.

You may know or have heard about people who live under very difficult conditions and are still able to maintain a state of stability, cheerfulness, and composure despite their challenging circumstances. For example, in January 2009, when I visited the monks and nuns from Plum Village at the European Institute of Applied Buddhism in Waldbröl, it was very cold in the large rooms of the huge building that they had taken on to renovate. I was in awe of their calm, cheerfulness, and humor as they went about planning seminars and courses while working and living in such uncomfortable quarters.

It's important and helpful to recognize these qualities of the awakened mind in others. There are often people in your immediate environment who have wonderful qualities that can help strengthen and support you on your path. If you recognize these people and are willing to be inspired by their positive energies, you can awaken these energies in yourself and connect with your own Buddha qualities. This is possible in every moment and in every situation of your life.

The following guided meditation can help you remember your own Buddha nature and the Buddha nature of all beings.

Breathing in, I know I'm breathing in.
Breathing out, I know I'm breathing out.

Breathing in, I connect with the energy of
mindfulness that exists in every cell of my body.
Breathing out, I feel inspired by the energy of
mindfulness in others.

*Breathing in, I connect with the energy of stability
that exists in every cell of my body.
Breathing out, I feel inspired by the energy of
stability in others.*

*Breathing in, I connect with the energy of joy that's
in every cell of my body.
Breathing out, I feel inspired by the energy of joy
in others.*

*Breathing in, I connect with the energy of
understanding that's in every cell of my body.
Breathing out, I feel inspired by the energy of
understanding in others.*

*Breathing in, I connect with the energy of open-
heartedness that's in every cell of my body.
Breathing out, I feel inspired by the energy of open-
heartedness in others.*

*Breathing in, I connect with the energy of generosity
in every cell of my body.
Breathing out, I feel inspired by the energy of
generosity in others.*

*Breathing in, I connect with the energy of
compassion in every cell of my body.*

Breathing out, I feel inspired by the energy of compassion in others.

Breathing in, I connect with the energy of calm in every cell of my body.
Breathing out, I feel inspired by the energy of calm in others.

Breathing in, I connect with the energy of awakening in every cell of my body.
Breathing out, I feel inspired by the energy of awakening in others.

Breathing in, I am aware of the preciousness of my spiritual practice.
Breathing out, I smile.

Acknowledgments

I WANT TO THANK all the teachers who have guided me and helped me to walk the path of understanding, love, and freedom. First, I'd like to thank my mother, who prayed with me every night when I was a child, and the kind Pastor Rücker in our Swabian village, who was in charge of my confirmation.

The two teachers I'm most devoted to are German-American Vipassana teacher Ruth Denison and Vietnamese Zen master Thich Nhat Hanh. I'm deeply grateful to both of them for their invaluable teachings. I also want to thank the entire Sangha of Plum Village —Thich Nhat Hanh's monastery and retreat center near Bordeaux, France—and all the nuns, monks, and laypeople there and at the European Institute of Applied Buddhism in Waldbröl near Cologne, Germany.

Many thanks to all my friends in our Source of

Compassion Sangha (Quelle des Mitgefühls) in Berlin and our small home Sangha at the Little Dharma Castle (Dharma Schlösschen).

A big thanks to my editor of the original German edition, Ursula Richard, who was a caring and wise guide during the time I was working on this book. I couldn't have done it without her. I also want to thank my good friend, Janina Egert, who has always supported me in many different ways.

About the Author

ANNABELLE ZINSER was born in 1948 in Swabia (Baden-Wuerttemberg, Germany). After she received her master's degree in history and political science, she worked as a social worker in Berlin. She trained as a massage therapist and yoga teacher and worked in both fields for many years.

In 1982, she attended her first meditation class with Sylvia Wetzel. While traveling in India in 1988, she participated in a Vipassana meditation retreat under the guidance of S.N. Goenka. Shortly afterwards, she met the German-American Vipassana teacher Ruth Denison at the Waldhaus am Laacher See near Koblenz, Germany. Annabelle studied with Ruth Denison for many years. She also received permission to teach the Dharma from Ruth Denison.

In 1992, she met Thich Nhat Hanh for the first time at the European Buddhist Congress in Berlin.

Since 2000, she has spent time at his monastery, Plum Village, near Bordeaux, France, on a regular basis. Annabelle entered the Order of Interbeing in 2003 and received the Lamp Transmission from Thich Nhat Hanh in 2004 to become a Dharma teacher, which authorized Annabelle to teach in his tradition.

Annabelle became a member of the Buddhist Academy Berlin-Brandenburg in 2001. In 2002, she began to build the Source of Compassion (Quelle des Mitgefühls), a Buddhist meditation center in the tradition of Plum Village in Berlin, Germany. She currently leads the Quelle des Mitgefühls meditation center.

Parallax Press, a nonprofit organization, publishes books on engaged Buddhism and the practice of mindfulness by Thich Nhat Hanh and other authors. For a copy of the catalog, please contact:

Parallax Press
P.O. Box 7355
Berkeley, CA 94707
Tel: (510) 525-0101
www.parallax.org

Related Titles from Parallax Press

Awakening Joy: 10 Steps to Happiness
James Baraz and Shoshana Alexander

Chanting from the Heart:
Buddhist Ceremonies and Daily Practices
Thich Nhat Hanh and the Monks
and Nuns of Plum Village

Happiness: Essential Mindfulness Practices
Thich Nhat Hanh

Love's Garden: A Guide to Mindful Relationships
Peggy Rowe Ward and Larry Ward

Making Space: Creating a Home Meditation Practice
Thich Nhat Hanh

Present Moment Wonderful Moment:
Mindfulness Verses for Daily Living
Thich Nhat Hanh

Ten Breaths to Happiness:
Touching Life in Its Fullness
Glen Schneider